MINUTE MIRACLES

THE PRACTICE OF LOGOSYNTHESIS®

INSPIRATION FROM REAL LIFE

DR. WILLEM LAMMERS

EDITED BY LARA CARDONA-MORISSET

Copyright ©Willem Lammers, 2019

The Origin of Logosynthesis®

Bristol House, Bahnhofstrasse 38, 7310 Bad Ragaz, Switzerland.

www.logosynthesis.net, info@logosynthesis.net

Version 01.09.2019

All rights reserved – most notably those of reproduction, distribution and translation.

Logosynthesis® and translations of this term are registered trademarks of the author, Willem Lammers, and may not be used without his express prior consent.

Clients' names and personal information have been changed.

ISBN-13: 9781095652428

Cover design and typesetting: Ian Dennis

TABLE OF CONTENTS

Foreword by Willem Lammers 6

Foreword by Lara Cardona-Morisset 8

INTRODUCTION 9

HEALTH AND ILLNESS 14

The Trauma Behind Smoking 14

Chronic Pain Release 16

Eat Everything on Your Plate 18

Regaining Womanhood 19

Coping with Cancer 20

Cardiac Surgery 22

Fear of a Medical Examination 23

Losing Weight 24

Eric's Eyes 26

SINGULAR TRAUMATIC EVENTS 28

Civil War Trauma 29

The End of a Dream 30

Processing a Car Crash 34

Thawing Frozen Grief 35

Frank Gets Attacked 38

Leaving the Baby Alone 39

TABLE OF CONTENTS

Domestic Violence 40

Celia's Guilt 42

Boarding the Wrong Train 43

Witnessing an Execution 44

Reconnecting with the Body 46

LIFE TRANSITIONS AND BELIEFS 50

Work and Success 51

Daisy's Belief 52

Rebecca Resolves a Belief 53

The Concept of Love 54

Judith's Guilt 54

The Child 56

Hannah Bids Farewell 58

The World as I Want It 60

Exploring the Void 62

The Pain Behind the Big Picture 64

Oliver's Tests at School 65

FAMILY OF ORIGIN 69

Losing Money, Becoming Poor 69

Driving 71

The Virtual Twin 72

I'm Not Good Enough	73
Her Place in the Sun	75
Given Away	76
She Should Have Been a Boy	77
The Girl with the Matches	79
I Don't Know my Boundaries	80
Showing Your Self	82
PHYSICAL ABUSE	**84**
Strangled by Grandfather	84
The Hands of My Father	86
Freedom from Slavery	87
Staying in Bed All Day	90
The Frozen Three-year-old	92
The Dark Shadow in the Light	94
Resolving Incompetence	96

FOREWORD BY
WILLEM LAMMERS

For many years I studied, practiced and taught guided change within the lines of traditional schools: coaching, counseling, supervision, psychology and psychotherapy. The discovery of Logosynthesis has profoundly altered my attitude towards this work. If you are living your own mission in this world, you know it often requires you to change your views, your concepts and your instruments completely.

Logosynthesis has shifted my focus from the psyche, with its emphasis on emotions, needs and inner states, to freeing the energy of Essence. In my own personal and spiritual development, specific themes appeared ahead of my conscious process, offering lessons or answers to questions not before thought of in my life. This method shows what's possible in this world, once our channels to Essence are open. Logosynthesis assists you in clearing those channels.

The principles of Logosynthesis are as profound as they are simple:

- We are life energy
- Life energy is either frozen or in flow
- Life energy either belongs to you, or it doesn't
- Words get energy moving.

When you start to think from the basis of those principles, after reading a book or taking an introductory course on Logosynthesis, you'll discover there is more to it.

This little book is intended to help you translate those simple principles into practical work. It contains a series of concrete examples from my own daily practice. Each chapter has been written immediately after a client session and was posted in the Logosynthesis Facebook group, to widen and deepen the skills and insights of people using Logosynthesis in their work.

If you want to know more about Logosynthesis, I recommend reading my books "Self-Coaching with Logosynthesis®. How the Power of Words Can Change Your Life" or "Logosynthesis –Healing with Words. A Handbook for the Healing Professions." You can also join Logosynthesis groups on Facebook or LinkedIn.

I want to thank all the people who contributed to this book, first of all Lara Cardona-Morisset, who patiently edited all my quickly written chapters and who kept asking the right questions. I also want to thank Ian Dennis, who just as calmly went through many versions of the cover and the typesetting, Pamela Burkhalter for her last-minute corrections, as well as all those who were present in the sessions described here, as clients or colleagues.

Bad Ragaz, at the foot of the Swiss Alps,
in the spring of 2019,

Willem Lammers

FOREWORD BY
LARA CARDONA-MORISSET

Being trained in Logosynthesis is like having a secret weapon in your pocket. It gives a feeling of invincibility, not because everything becomes perfect, but because everything becomes workable. There's a wonderful realization that the inner battle has turned to peace. No more forcing yourself to overcome difficult things, mental gymnastics to solve problems that appear insurmountable, or battling feelings of anxiety that won't go away.

Instead, there is the gentle, persuasive, kind way of working with Logosynthesis. Looking deeply for the roots of suffering and dissolving them with words. No longer is it necessary to confront or avoid. With this tool, you can face your problems and turn them into solutions with the application of three simple sentences.

By extension, working with others using Logosynthesis feels to me like a profound expression of love. The ability to support other people while they face their own suffering and dissolve its frozen structures gives a feeling of joy and inner strength. Going deep diving alongside another into the unknown darkness until you find the cause of the pain that has made itself known.

It has been an honor to edit these case studies. All of them are exhibits of the same truth: Allow the sentences to work, and the world lays itself at your feet. It then reveals the joy behind the frozen energy dissolving in front of you.

INTRODUCTION

If you are familiar with Logosynthesis, you'll know its application always follows a similar path:

- First, you build a solid working alliance with the person in front of you. You must reach the level of trust necessary for a person to leave their comfort zone on a trip into unknown territory. Your clients must know they're in good hands and be confident that the tools and techniques you use will help them on their life path. They're not questioning your methods: they trust you in the way they trust their family dentist or their car mechanic.

- Once your client feels welcomed, you start to explore the reasons why they have come to you and create a space to let them open up and tell their story. This is a precious moment for many people; they meet you in moments of suffering and tend to feel a profound relief when someone is really listening.

- As they tell the story, you start to listen for cues that can guide your work into the next stage. How does the client describe the world they live in? How big are the power and influences they experience? Are they able to think clearly, or are they caught in memories, fantasies and beliefs? Which emotions show up, and how do these guide your client's behavior?

- Once the client has begun to feel comfortable with the setting and with you as a guide, you can start to explore what is behind the world as the client is perceiving it. What is triggering the emotions and physical sensations the client is feeling? What is in the present, what is hidden in history? What are their fantasies about the future? You carefully guide a transition from the presented problem to a world that has never before been explored.

- Now you find the level of distress the client is experiencing regarding the presented issue, and you move from listening to the story as a whole to explore essential aspects: Which people, times, and places were significant in the creation of this distress? Many complaints that appear firmly related to the present are in fact deeply rooted in painful events of the past.

- When you have found out what is triggering the client to feel as he feels, you start designing the Logosynthesis sentences for the trigger of the unpleasant experiences. You only offer those sentences if the client has reached a receptive stage in which they are open for you and for all the methods you will want to use to resolve the client's issues. This openness is located somewhere between dependency and resistance: If a client entirely depends on you, they are probably reluctant to take responsibility themselves, and if they're resistant, they won't allow the sentences to work as designed.

- Each sentence contains a label X, which stands for the frozen perception of a memory, a fantasy or a belief. As a rule, that means you're able to see, hear, sense, smell or taste X. X *never* contains an emotion or a reaction to a perception. For many professionals, this is somewhat unusual, because traditional schools of guided change tend to focus more on emotional reactions than on the perception of the events that trigger those emotions.

- Before you continue, you make sure you have a glass of water ready. It often happens that a client feels tired, dizzy or nauseous. These are usually signs of intense processing and disappear when the client drinks water.

- When the client is ready for a step into the unknown, you offer them the first sentence and ask them to repeat it. You provide it in small chunks – this is not a memory exercise – you let the client repeat that part and take the time to let each sentence sink in. In time you'll recognize the signs that the sentence has finished processing, and you offer the next one.

- The first sentence is "I retrieve all my energy, bound up in (this perception) X and take it to the right place in my Self." You say that sentence in parts, and you invite the client to repeat each part after you. In the beginning, this may be unfamiliar, but in fact, it's not much different from a family physician asking a patient to say "Ah."

- After the client has said the sentence, you take the time for a working pause, in which they process the information that has been given to their system through the sentence. In this pause, different reactions are possible, from yawning and relaxation to deep emotions. If emotions show up, you will let the client repeat the sentence without interrupting the cycle.

- The same procedure is applied to the second sentence: "I remove all non-me energy, related to X, from all of my cells, all of my body and my personal space, and send it to where it truly belongs." Again followed by a working pause.

- The third sentence follows the same pattern: "I retrieve all my energy, bound up in all my reactions to (this perception) X and take it to the right place in my Self."

- After the series of three sentences and their working pauses, you create a space for the experience, and invite the client to share their process, usually with the help of an open question, such as "What's happening now?" This will reveal if the current issue has been resolved or if additional exploration and processing is needed.

- If the level of distress has been sufficiently reduced and nothing new comes up, the next step of the process is future-pacing: You invite the client to imagine the future to determine if the distress experienced it has completely disappeared. If this is not the case, a new cycle starts, focusing on the issue that showed up in the future pacing. If everything is resolved and no longer causes distress, you can close the cycle and explore what else needs to be done in the session.

The more you work with Logosynthesis, on your own issues or with clients, the easier it becomes to apply the standard protocol of Logosynthesis, the Basic Procedure. The case examples in this book are meant to provide you with a deeper understanding of this process. If you look at the separate chapters with the above procedure in mind, you will discover there are endless variations possible, but they all can be reduced to the above steps.

For many trainees and Practitioners, it is an ongoing challenge to let go of existing skills and knowledge of coaching, counseling and psychotherapy. In Logosynthesis it is often unnecessary to linger with intense emotions: The search for the trigger of these emotions and its neutralization will bring faster relief than the most empathic form of staying with them.

It is also not necessary to interpret events or offer a new frame of reference to help a client understand what is happening in their life or how to enact change. As soon as the power of words has done its fantastic work, many clients are well able to find this new understanding themselves, to their own surprise and to mine.

Working with Logosynthesis is often about thinking less and doing less. I tend to say: "As a Practitioner in Logosynthesis you must be lazy, stupid and slow." You don't need much effort, because the words themselves will do the work. You don't need to think or interpret on behalf of the client, because the client will regain their own thinking power in the course of the process. You don't need any speed in your interventions, on the contrary: You can sit on your hands until the processing pause has ended, and the client reconnects with you.

HEALTH AND ILLNESS

Illness is as paradoxical as life itself. Life and death are aspects of the same process, and the same is true for health and illness. Illness creates discomfort, dis-ease: fear, anger, pain and sadness, in yourself and in others: a confrontation with fantasies and expectations, with what life could have been, should have been, could be and should be.

In this interaction with existential issues, Logosynthesis can play an important role in clarifying your position. Identify the desires, wishes, expectations and fantasies around the illness that has appeared in your life. Find the archaic images and voices associated with them and neutralize or dissolve them with the Logosynthesis sentences. Once your energy isn't bound in fantasies anymore, it will be freely available to help you heal the illness or to turn the disease into a condition you can live with. The life you chose was never meant to be perfect.

THE TRAUMA
BEHIND SMOKING

Alexander wanted to quit smoking. He had agreed to not smoke since last night, and now had strong cravings for a cigarette. He had been smoking on and off for years, and recently had started again. When I asked him *why* he smoked, he answered that he felt a need to smoke. This "need" manifested as a sensation in his chest, described as a "sucking force." I asked him if he believed that this "force" indicated a need to smoke a cigarette. Alexander confirmed that he did.

I told him that I had my doubts about that hypothesis and carefully guided him back in time to the first occasion of this "sucking force."

He remembered a situation as a seven-year-old, being in the hospital in which he had felt alone. His parents weren't there, and he reported that this was the first time that he had this feeling, long before he touched his first cigarette. When I went further back in time with him, another memory showed up in which he awoke from anesthesia after surgery, and again no one was there. His throat felt dry. Alexander neutralized this memory with the help of the Logosynthesis sentences and felt a great relief. Then I guided him back to the situation at the hospital at the age of seven, and he saw himself standing at the door of the room, waiting for his mother. After two rounds with sentence 1, this image disappeared.

The intensity of the symptom in his chest had decreased, but it hadn't fully resolved itself. We were at the end of our time, so I gave him a last round for "the hidden perception that leads to this sensation in my chest," and then "the sucking force" went away.

Alexander had learned that the symptom in his chest didn't mean that he needed a cigarette. That feeling was associated with an early childhood trauma that was reactivated every once in a while. Smoking a cigarette made the feeling disappear – for a limited time. Nicotine needs 10 seconds to reach the brain and soothe the memory. Logosynthesis needs 30 seconds to peel off a layer of the underlying traumatic structure. Alexander now prefers to practice the latter.

In the lunch break after the session, there was no need to smoke a cigarette. In the future Alexander will have more work to do when other aspects of a traumatic childhood show up: He was hospitalized four times as a child, and this probably wasn't his only experience of being abandoned.

I often see a connection between early experiences of abandonment and addictive behavior. When we access these traumatic events and neutralize them, the need for substances and actions to manage the painful state decrease.

MEMORIES
PARENTS
HEALTH AND ILLNESS

CHRONIC PAIN RELEASE

Eve has suffered chronic spinal pain for many years. It had started at age 15 after several sports accidents, and had become worse after three car accidents, especially after the last one, which was 6-7 years ago. Since then she had lived with chronic pain. In this session she also reported a pain in the heart region, with an intensity of 8 and a degree of emotional distress of 6 on a scale of 0–10. She also had a pain around her torso, with an intensity of 4.

After the last car accident, Eve had been on an odyssey through the medical world and alternative health care, trying everything from morphine treatment to craniosacral therapy. Impressed by her story, I asked what she expected from this demonstration, and she answered: "A change." This sounded like a realistic goal; Eve had been disappointed often enough to be firmly rooted in reality.

I asked her if she had ever worked on the trauma of the accidents. She said she hadn't, and later she told me that this was the deeper reason she had applied for the course. A direction for the work became clear: We could at least work on the trauma of the last car accident, as this was the moment when the pain had become stronger.

I asked Eve to describe the circumstances of the accident. She was riding in the car with her husband, full of energy, enjoying the day and preparing to buy a kitchen for their newly built home. After a right turn, they collided suddenly into a row of cars that had slowed down behind a tractor. I asked her about the connection between the collision and the pain, and she said that she had felt the crash in her breast. It also seemed to her that the shock had been stored there in some way.

I instructed Eve to re-experience the moment of the accident, and she reported how her breath stopped. Then she said something strange "I see myself being shot out of the window of the car." I gave her three sentences for this image and – lo and behold – the intensity of the pain reduced to 2 and the emotional distress to zero. She stood up and walked throughout the room, enjoying her body, telling me she felt two inches taller.

I asked Eve to again enter the memory of the crash, and this time she felt her body leaving the car before the crash. I offered her the first sentence for this imagined experience, and

Minute Miracles 17

then she said: "I'm leaving this hurt, wounded, violated body. That's not the real me." In the last sequence, I gave her the sentences for the energy bound up in the perception of her body and of the environment at the time of the accident.

After this, a slight pain was left in her shoulder, which she can continue to treat herself. The pain in the heart region had gone. Eve was happy.

ACCIDENT
HEALTH AND ILLNESS
MEMORIES

EAT EVERYTHING ON YOUR PLATE

Andy is 65 and always feels obligated to eat everything on his plate, even though he is already full. This is not because he likes the food; he feels uncomfortable if something is left on his plate. He also eats anything his wife doesn't finish on her own plate.

Exploring the roots of this reaction, he recounts that his mother used to warm up and serve a second time to them any food a child in the family refused to eat. Both parents reinforced the ban on leaving anything on the plate. In a mapping, Andy places markers for his parents and himself in space at a close distance. Most of the energy is bound in the representation of his mother, who forbade him to leave anything on his plate.

Andy then says the sentences for this representation of his mother. Immediately after he feels independent, with more freedom and lightness. Imagining his wife offering him her leftovers, he kindly refuses. He also has no problem visualizing leaving food on his plate when he has eaten enough. He is easily able to recognize that the rules he learned were very relevant in the post-war era, when eating everything available was an economic necessity. He is also now aware that times have changed.

▪
HEALTH AND ILLNESS
PARENTS
MEMORIES

REGAINING WOMANHOOD

Thirty years ago Mireille suffered a traumatic sports accident: She was in a training program; the only woman in a group of men. In an exercise, she had to jump over a pole to land on a trampoline. She was successful in the first attempt, but during the second attempt she was overcome with fear. During this attempt, as she jumped, Mireille landed directly upon the pole, which pierced her body, deeply entering her vagina and cutting her uterus. When it happened, her first thought was: "I'm not a woman anymore." After the accident, she underwent many surgical operations, but never regained her former health. Now, after many years, she still suffered from pain in her knees and hips, and a feeling of instability in her body. It was a shock when her daughter, an osteopath, told her that had she been treated with osteopathy after the accident, she wouldn't have all these symptoms.

Asked to isolate the most distressful element of the story she had just recounted, Mireille didn't mention the accident itself, but her conclusion: "I'm not a woman anymore." This was as stressful as her daughter's statement about what could have happened had she been treated earlier. As the conclusion about herself as a woman was more closely linked to the accident, I chose to work with that. After three sentences on this belief, she said: "It's not true. I am a woman." When I gave her the sentences for the wish to have been treated earlier, her face softened and her body visibly relaxed. Walking around, she noticed that standing and walking had become easier.

Here I decided to address the accident itself: I asked her to say the Logosynthesis sentences for the energy bound in the representation of the pole that had penetrated her body. As a result, she relaxed even more deeply, and for the first time in 30 years could walk without pain. Her face looked ten years younger, and she beamed with joy.

HEALTH AND ILLNESS
WORK
ACCIDENT

COPING WITH CANCER

"I want to get rid of this illness." Conny, in her fifties, looked at me with eyes full of determination. She had recently been diagnosed with cancer and had undergone surgery. For the moment she didn't show any symptoms, but the illness still impacted her life greatly. I answered that I didn't have ways to cure cancer, but that I could assist her in identifying and resolving limiting patterns related to the illness.

In the following interview, she declared that she didn't want to surrender to the medical system, she'd rather "feed the fish." Conny told a story about how she had taken care of her mother until the bitter end, dying of cancer in a hospital where she was being treated like an object. She described a scene in a ward, where her mother was dying and in pain and being shoved around in her bed on wheels. When Conny protested against that treatment, the physician in charge responded with arrogance.

She said the Logosynthesis sentences for this scene, and tears of grief showed up. She said: "I can't change anything." In the next cycle, she said the sentences for "the wish to change the situation of my mother." Now she visibly relaxed and remembered with a smile how she had prevented further unnecessary pain for her mother by confronting the physician.

The memory of her mother dying now felt neutral, and when I guided her back to the issue she presented at the beginning, Conny shared a fear for the future. She wasn't afraid of dying, but she was horrified by the idea of suffering. In the third cycle, I gave her three sentences for this image of herself suffering. When she had finished this process, the horror was gone, and she said: "I can manage whatever may happen."

■
HEALTH AND ILLNESS
PARENTS
MEMORIES

CARDIAC SURGERY

Luis is 70 and recently underwent cardiac surgery that involved a long period of rehabilitation. He has an extreme fear of having to go through that again, and there is a chance of this happening.

In a long session, we looked at and processed many aspects of his current life. The most significant one was the moment he's waiting for surgery, when the doctor came and explained the procedure. He used words like "We have the best team for you" and "We're going to disconnect you and put you on an artificial respirator." When Luis told that story, he froze in terror. The idea that he could be disconnected again and be "sent into a black hole" was more than he could bear.

I gave him three sentences for "the belief that I am the body that's disconnected." The working pauses were deeply silent and lasted several minutes. Then the panic was gone.

In times of physical pain and trouble, we tend to identify with our bodies and disconnect from Essence. Medical science tends to support that identification, because the body is the center of its focus. If you want to feel seen by your doctor, it's easiest if you tune in to their frame of reference. In this process, all involved create a reality together in which a whole human being is reduced to an organ or their physical body.

You are more than that physical body. You're Essence, an immortal being, beyond space and time.

■
ESSENCE
HEALTH AND ILLNESS
SOCIOENERGETIC FIELDS

FEAR OF A MEDICAL EXAMINATION

Pierre, a young man with Crohn's disease, regularly needs to undergo a colonoscopy and kept postponing his appointment for this annoying examination. The last one had been done five years ago and it was overdue. In the initial interview, it turned out that Pierre's resistance was not related to the examination itself, this takes place under anesthesia, but to the tedious preparation in which one has to drink liters of an unpleasant smelling liquid. He also feared the repetition of an earlier situation when he had thrown up several bottles of this fluid and had to start the preparations all over again.

Pierre's level of distress while imagining preparing for the colonoscopy at the beginning of the session was extremely high, a 10 on the 0–10 scale. In the application of the Logosynthesis sentences, Pierre neutralized a range of perceptual triggers one by one:

- The terrible taste of the saline solution he had to drink.
- The pink color of the saline solution in the bottles.
- The visual markers on the bottles, showing how much he had to drink every 15 minutes.
- The smell of the saline solution in his nose.
- The kinesthetic experience of his stomach feeling like it was going to explode from the fluid.
- The dissociated image of himself vomiting out a wave of the fluid.
- The image of the yellow floor and the white doctor's coat after regaining consciousness.

After these seven rounds Pierre's feet felt warm, and he perceived the colors in the room more intensely. When I asked him to imagine making an appointment and going through the preparations, we had to do one last round on the image of the monitor and the colonoscopy tube in the examination room. Then he said: "I feel tired; now I'm going to sleep while they're doing the procedure." It turned out that the colonoscopy itself was associated with a deep feeling of relaxation as a result of the anesthesia.

HEALTH AND ILLNESS
IMAGES
MEMORIES

LOSING WEIGHT

Many people try to lose weight through reduction of their food intake. Usually this doesn't work, at least not in the long run. The reason is simple: One part of the client's energy system wants to lose weight – a punishing, repressive introject – and another part feels threatened if food intake is reduced. Dieting is often limited to reduction or change in food intake and doesn't take this threat into account.

However, if the threatened part isn't treated, no diet will ever lead to permanent weight loss. Therefore, in working with Logosynthesis, you start with exploring what a client feels when they feel hungry. The experience connected with hunger has sensory as well as emotional components. In a session Will, a strong, tall and heavy man, identified "hunger" as a pressure around his head, combined with a feeling of insecurity.

Through flash questions we found a disturbing memory at age 2. Little Will was alone in his room and felt utterly insecure. After the sentences for the frozen memory, the energy level rose, and he felt anger. I explained to him that anger results from the belief that a need must be fulfilled, while in real life this need was not fulfilled. As a next step he said the sentences for the mother he would have liked to have had, but never had.

After this, Will felt fear, which turned out to be a fear that Mommy would never come back. Saying the sentences for this fantasy, the fear dissolved, and we returned to the starting point of the session, the hunger feeling. The insecurity had disappeared from the sensation, and he felt a steel band around his head and between his ears.

When we tracked this feeling in his history, Will remembered a situation as a seven-year-old, in which his father had comforted him. Something had happened to him, which was still covered by the memory of Father. After the suggestion to step back in time, Will discovered a memory in which he was bullied by three other children. His sister also played a role in this event.

This memory was also neutralized with the Logosynthesis sentences, and returning to the sensation of hunger, there was no distress. He felt his body could take in food, but totally without the unpleasant sensations that had accompanied this feeling of hunger. Now he could imagine fasting for a longer period without the stress that had foiled his earlier attempts. We now both are curious how this is going to work out. It makes so much sense to look at losing weight from this perspective. If a client has felt bad, hungry and abandoned at the same time, usually the reconnection to the caretakers has been associated with food intake. Sweets are "deserved" after letting the parents have their night out or weekend off. During dieting, this learned sensation of hunger may invite the client to be that brave again, paving the way for the next sugar shot: "Now I deserve it!"

HEALTH AND ILLNESS
PARENTS
FAMILY OF ORIGIN

ERIC'S EYES

Eric is an older gentleman with extensive experience in Logosynthesis. For the last six months, he has suffered from a blind spot in his right eye, in the center of the retina, the fovea. The ophthalmologist has told him that he cannot see there because of a blood clot sitting behind the fovea. His peripheral view is OK. The clot can easily be seen as a black spot of 2–3 cm on a large X-ray of the eye, and there is a 40% chance that his left eye could also be affected. Eric was afraid, as you can imagine.

I decided to introduce Eric to my Logosynthesis Simonton protocol and invited him to think of something this blood clot was like. He immediately associated it with a stain of tomato sauce on a clean white shirt. Since Eric is always impeccably dressed, this stain generated a 7 on a SUD scale. I now gave him the Logosynthesis sentences for "this tomato stain on my shirt." After processing the stain this way, it disappeared from his white shirt and the level of distress triggered by the metaphor went to zero.

From here I addressed the X-ray photograph of the eye that Eric had seen in the ophthalmologist's consulting room. This image can also be considered a metaphor. I had him say the sentences for the black spot in the center, and as a result, the spot turned pink. After a second cycle, this pink form became a thin line, just a contour of the original black spot. A third cycle of the sentences made the thin line disappear completely.

When I asked him to explore the state of his right eye again, he told me that he could now see a more or less transparent contour of me, whereas before there had just been a black spot. I let him drink water and take a 30-minute break for a walk outside to let the process continue. After his return we explored his field of view again. Now it had widened from the left towards the center. Before the sentences Eric could only see the bookshelves in my consulting room, on the right in his peripheral vision, and he had not even been able to see the flip chart beside my chair. Now he was able to see it.

There are many details in this protocol that can only be taught in training, but this may give you an idea how to treat issues that may seem purely "physical." It's important to think in energy concepts from the beginning, and a blood clot is one more manifestation of frozen energy.

HEALTH AND ILLNESS
IMAGES
WORKING ALLIANCE

SINGULAR **TRAUMATIC** EVENTS

The Self is Essence manifested in the world of form, and it has a mission: to teach, to learn, to explore, to discover. On entering the world, you are a coherent energy system in flow, equipped with a body and a mind as vehicles, instruments, tools in the service if its mission. These vehicles need development and maintenance: for the body food, drink, shelter, movement, rest, practice and for the mind information, constancy, variety, attention, support, respect. If the needs connected to certain stages of development are not sufficiently met, the development of the Self is arrested, and the awareness of body and mind overwhelms the awareness of the Self's true nature and mission: trauma.

In trauma, parts of the energy of the Original Self are split off and freeze as separate energy structures: first order dissociation. These frozen structures contain a limited form of consciousness that's locked in the moment of the trauma and disconnected from the awareness of the Original Self and its corresponding Essence. The frozen consciousness in these structures can be reactivated in reaction to similar or associated events. Because this reactivation can be extremely painful, the Self creates another layer of energy structures, which protect the Self against the trauma: second order dissociation. The Adult Self is what's left of the Original Self after multiple experiences of dissociation. Our task in Logosynthesis is to restore the flow of energy in the frozen structures and heal the Self, to make it whole again.

CIVIL WAR TRAUMA

Jonathan, a Catholic priest, still suffered from traumatic memories of a civil war situation he was involved in nine years ago. He arrived at a site where people had been wounded and killed, and where police officers were acting inappropriately. He was shocked by the injustice he saw around him and wanted to support the people in his parish.

After he had described the situation, treatment focused on two traumatic images. The first one was seeing a woman he knew, lying on the street, not knowing if she was alive or dead. The second image was a police officer stepping on the head of a man lying on the ground. Both images were neutralized with one round of the Logosynthesis sentences.

After the processing of these traumatic images, he became quieter, but there remained distress about the injustice of the situation. The police should have protected those citizens, but instead they had become violent.

I asked how he had wished the police had behaved, and then offered him the sentences for this wish. In the third sentence, I used the following form: "I retrieve all my energy bound up in all my reactions to the fact that this wish was not fulfilled." This sentence took time to process, but then he looked at me with a smile on his face. He was able to recognize that this had been nine years ago now, and that the situation in the country had improved since then. Life is not always as we wish it to be. Binding energy in desires and wishes limits our potential to do what we can.

WISHES AND DESIRES
WORK
TRAUMA

THE END
OF A DREAM

Jenny and Jack, a recently retired couple, had spent the last four years creating a new home for themselves in the South of France. Jack was a retired businessman, Jenny an artist, and together they constructed their dream home. Three weeks ago, the dream was destroyed by a terrible incident. At four in the morning, Jenny was awoken by the sound of footsteps on the gravel path outside. The cat on her bed jumped out of the window in panic. When she got up and went towards the door of the bedroom she heard loud hammering, as if someone was trying to break through the front door. She realized that there were several people attempting to break in.

In the meantime, her husband had also woken and asked what was going on, and when his wife screamed from the top of her lungs he knew something was wrong. He went back to the bedroom, retrieved the gun he kept there, and went outside to look. A tall man dressed all in black appeared, his face fully covered by a balaclava. To Jack he looked like Darth Vader, the Star Wars character. To Jenny he was a giant black monster.

The man in black held a shiny metallic object in his hands. He was not alone, there were two others just as tall, and the situation seemed dire. Suddenly the burglar brought the shiny object upwards. Jack, well trained in the military, shot immediately to defend himself and Jenny. He hit the man in black, and all three members of the gang fled, climbing over the wall.

In his description of the shooting, Jack used an interesting expression: "The shot was fired." He didn't say: "I shot the man." His military brain had taken over automatically and pulled the trigger without conscious thought. The couple now found themselves wrapped in a deafening silence. The threat was over; the whole sequence had barely taken six minutes. Now they could call for help, and when the officers arrived they discovered the dead body of the burglar near the wall.

Jack was taken to the police station. He was interrogated repeatedly the next day. The investigators soon decided that he had killed the burglar in self-defense and set him free, without legal consequences. Jack was even allowed to return to his home country. The man shot was the boss of a gang, known to the police. The other two men could not be found.

Then the nightmare began. Jenny was in a permanent state of panic, while Jack did his best to remain calm. They changed the locks in their permanent home in Switzerland, installed security cameras throughout and did everything else they could think of to prevent another attack. On a rational level they were vaguely aware that their reactions were exaggerated, and that something else was going on with them. A highly unusual painful event leads to specific reactions, in which your organism tries to process the experienced situation. These reactions can be a combination of re-experiencing, avoidance, and hyperarousal. All three could be easily identified in Jack and Jenny.

At this point, after reading my book, telling their stories and receiving the information, Jack and Jenny seemed to feel safe enough to begin processing the event with Logosynthesis. I asked them: "Who of you is suffering the most?" They both agreed it was Jenny. If Jack's suffering was less visible: He seemed to be in control and was able to support Jenny in her pain.

I distilled three key moments or perceptions in Jenny's experience:

1. The noise of the steps on the gravel path.

2. The hammering on the front door.

3. The image of the "Black Monster."

None were dominant, so I took a chronological approach, treating one after the other. Because of the lack of safety Jenny experienced during those traumatic moments, I added an additional safety component by saying the Logosynthesis sentences on her behalf. Three times the cycle started with a maximum distress score of 10, and three times the 10 reduced to zero. In the last cycle, I had Jenny say the sentences herself, to give her more power in the process. After every cycle, Jenny smiled, but she also expressed doubts it would hold.

Jenny initially had shared feelings of deep grief. They had planned to grow old in that beautiful house, hosting family and friends. This time Jenny sounded quieter and more rational, being able to reflect instead of being locked in the grief of the loss.

At the next session, the couple entered smiling, and Jenny told me that she had tried to activate the memory of the man in black. She hadn't been able to, and the memory of the noise was completely gone. For the first time since the incident, she had slept through the night without interruption. She was astonished. I said that I couldn't explain it logically, but that I didn't mind: I summarized the energy model from my Logosynthesis self-coaching book in a few sentences, to frame their experience.

For Jack the last session had dealt with the loss of his paradise, and this was still bothering him as well as Jenny. They were in the process of selling the house, because they didn't want to expose themselves to the risk that the robber gang would come after them. This was a realistic fear, which I didn't interfere with.

Jenny was very clear about losing a place of deep togetherness with friends and family. When I asked Jack for an image representing that paradise, he described how he was sitting at a table with his computer, with a view of the Mediterranean. The level of distress about the loss of this magnificent view was a 7. I gave him the sentences for the view, with a modification of the third one: "I retrieve all my energy bound up in all my reactions to the fact that I won't have this view anymore, and take it to the right place in myself." After a few minutes of processing, in which Jack was visibly moved, he was able to find his usual, optimistic stance, realizing that such things happen in life.

I did another cycle with Jenny about her fear of the dark since the incident. Returning home, the darkness around their permanent home had reactivated the memory of that tragic incident, and this had become a secondary trauma. This was neutralized with one cycle of the sentences for the perception of the darkness. Logosynthesis is very well equipped to treat a Type I PTSD, the sequelae of a one-time traumatic incident.

▩
ROMANCE
PARTNERSHIP
TRAUMA

PROCESSING A CAR CRASH

Anastasia had been involved in a traffic accident a few years ago. She had driven through a yellow traffic light and woken up in the hospital. She had been wounded in the crash and since then suffered from whiplash. She had hit the rearview mirror with her head, suffered a wound to her left leg, and a separated shoulder. The dominant symptom was the pain in her neck, with a SUD level of 6, the scar in her leg hurt as well.

She applied the Logosynthesis sentences on the memory of touching the rearview mirror and everything else that had touched her. The SUDs for the pain in her neck went from 6 to 3. At this moment a belief showed up: "It shouldn't have happened." I gave her the sentences for this belief, with the modified third phrase: "I retrieve all my energy bound up in all my reactions to the fact that it happened." Anastasia then said: "I'm here and it's over."

Then other beliefs showed up: "I didn't deserve it", "Whiplash doesn't go away" and then an older one: "Physically, I'll always have pain." The latter one was connected to memories of her father beating her and she said: "The pain always comes." I gave her the sentences for this belief, and the SUDs went from 3 to 2. Anastasia sat straighter now and started to move her head and neck to free herself from the strain of all those years. Then another belief showed up: "You need pain to be taken care of." One more round of the Logosynthesis sentences, and the pain was gone: in her neck as well as in her leg. The phrase "Whiplash doesn't go away" had lost all significance to her.

ACCIDENT
BELIEFS
HEALTH AND ILLNESS

THAWING FROZEN GRIEF

François, a big strong man, was still grieving for the loss of his sister, who had died in a traffic accident in France in 1979. For 34 years he had suffered in silence; now it seemed the right time to continue his life's path. In tears, he told the story of a dramatic week, how a police officer showed up at this front door and delivered the news that would change his life. After the police officer left, François had been in a state of shock. Finally, he had found the courage to inform his parents of his sister's death, first his father, then his mother.

In the days that followed, he went to France to see his sister's body and to arrange her transport to his country. When he arrived at the hospital, a nurse advised him he'd better not look at his dead sister: She had been trapped in the car and her body was badly disfigured. He decided not to view the body.

Here stalled François's story. His voice had sounded as if the fatal accident had happened yesterday. His grief touched me deeply, and I took the time to let his story sink in. I had to do something, but what? There was so much material that I could begin with, I could help him process each single event in that traumatic week, but that didn't seem right. There had to be a single key intervention to end the grief process at once.

When is the time for a final farewell? After people have seen the dead relative. François had not seen his sister after she passed and hadn't had an opportunity to say goodbye. The nurse had blocked the grieving process, paradoxically caused by her wish to protect him against reality. Thus, there was no picture of this reality: 34 years after her death François remembered his dearly loved sister as a cheerful 24-year-old, full of plans, full of life. On a subconscious level, he had a repressed fantasy of what his sister must have looked like when she died in that car wreck that night.

This was the key to the solution. I gave François the Logosynthesis phrases, which he repeated, and I gave him the time to let them sink in:

1. I retrieve all my energy, bound up in the image of my sister I've never seen, and take it back to the right place in my Self.

2. I remove all non-me energy related to this image, from all of my cells, from all of my body and my personal space and send it to where it truly belongs.

3. I retrieve all my energy, bound up in all my frozen reactions to the image of my sister I've never seen, and take it to the right place in my self.

The effect of the sentences was dramatic. Initially François cried softly, tears running down his cheeks. After a few minutes he became silent. I asked him what had happened, and with a dull voice he said, "Now I can recognize that my sister is gone." Now he knew their roads had parted on that day in 1979. He felt a great emptiness. Then he described a small image of his sister, which he saw up high in the room, on his left side, and he pointed to the beams of the attic where we worked.

Now I gave François the Logosynthesis sentences for this small image. After the second sentence, while the energy of his sister was leaving his personal space, he wept for minutes without holding back, which was heartbreaking. This was the real grief, saying goodbye to a life with his sister. After the third sentence François was quiet again, but this time the silence was different, there was a relief: The agony was over, everything had found a place after 34 years. Now I could talk to him about the fact that every person has their own way of life, that those roads meet, that we walk together for a while and then split up. This interpretation seemed to help François to create an order in his experience, and we were able to close the session. In the last minute of the session I had tears in my eyes as well.

Two days later, François's wife Nadine told the group that in the morning after the session she had been awake early and had looked at her sleeping husband. In her words, François normally looks like "one of those dogs whose head seems to consist of folds." That morning all his wrinkles were gone. François said he felt reborn.

IMAGES
ACCIDENT
LIFE TRANSITIONS

FRANK GETS ATTACKED

Frank is a successful sales manager. During his first session with me, he talked about a trip that he'd taken through South America many years ago. In Caracas, a criminal gang had enticed him into a dark bar with the promise of free drinks. When he entered the bar, he was mugged by a group of women. Only a combination of luck and dexterity allowed him to make a dive for freedom. As he broke away, the gang member who had enticed him into the bar was talking to two police officers out on the street. The same thing happened to his friend a few minutes later when he went into the bar to look for Frank.

This incident was too much for Frank: being robbed – by women – while the police officers had a relaxed discussion with one of the gang members had a serious impact on his life. He was diagnosed with post-traumatic stress disorder, which manifested in panic attacks, especially if he entered an unfamiliar bar. His memories of the bar in Venezuela were then reactivated and he experienced intense physical and emotional reactions, causing him to quickly retreat.

Frank would have simply avoided bars in future if this had been his only problem. But he was also no longer able to approach people in a relaxed manner at work – a significant handicap for a manager working in customer service.

The cause of his panic emerged during the session; an unconscious fantasy while he was in that bar: "They're going to kill me!" A mental video clip played of being beaten to death with baseball bats. This fantasy was reactivated whenever he entered an unfamiliar bar or met new people. Frank responded with fear, rage and panic even when he was in a friendly environment.

The video in his mind changed after he applied Logosynthesis. Frank now remembered how he celebrated his misadventures' successful outcome with his friend, on a terrace under the Caracas sun.

TRAUMA
IMAGES
FANTASIES

LEAVING THE BABY ALONE

Ten years ago, Ginny's then one-year-old daughter had fallen seriously ill and was hospitalized after she had left the house with her husband to go to a musical for the first time in months. Although she was reluctant to leave home because her child had a fever, she opted for the evening out with her husband while her sister took care of the toddler.

During intermission, she called home and her sister told her that her child's condition had worsened, she had been taken to the hospital. Ginny left the theater in a panic, followed by her husband. During the 90-minute drive to the hospital, Ginny was beside herself. In the end, the situation ended happily; the child recovered quickly.

Now, almost ten years later, the event still made Ginny cry. It became clear that she had wished to be there when her daughter became seriously ill for the first time. She also had a fear that her daughter would die. The sentences resolved both this unfulfilled wish and this fantasy of her daughter dying.

▪

HEALTH AND ILLNESS
CHILDREN
WISHES AND DESIRES

DOMESTIC VIOLENCE

Heidi wanted to get rid of a past relationship. After seven years with ups and downs, she had finally managed to end the relationship, but she still felt guilty and ashamed. I asked her what the worst incident in those years had been. Of course, there were many, but the following one was the worst.

She had bought tickets for a planned trip with this partner, and he suddenly refused to go on the journey with her. When she told him that she wanted him to pay for his ticket, he became angry, took his iPad and smashed it on the ground. Heidi reacted by going to her desk and writing an email to her partner's psychiatrist. While she was writing, she noticed something moving next to her. She thought her partner had opened the refrigerator, but when she looked up, she saw him lifting the TV above his head. He then threw it with all his might, and it exploded with an enormous bang.

The story contained several aspects to work on. In the interview it became clear that the worst moment was when the TV exploded, and that the most significant aspect was the sound that came with the explosion. More than two years later, Heidi still rated that bang an 8 on the 0–10 distress scale.

I gave her the sentences for the auditory trigger, "the bang." In the working pause she kept her eyes open, staring at me. Normally, a client stops looking at me when I turn away my gaze, but she didn't; therefore I asked her to close her eyes. I had her repeat the first sentence a few times until she felt safe enough to keep her eyes closed, and then the process went quickly. The SUDs for "the bang" went from 8 to 3, and the preceding incident with the iPad became unimportant. When I made a joke about it Heidi could laugh.

I asked her if she got rid of the relationship and she laughed, but then something curious happened. She said, "I can't get rid of him," which she then corrected to, "I don't want to get rid of him." I challenged her and asked her "can't or don't want to?" I told her that if you want something, there must be a choice involved, so both statements cannot be true at the same time.

The strength of the negative belief "I can't get rid of him" was an 8. The representation of it was visual, the text written in an arc slightly above her head in front of her. When she said the sentences for this statement, she quietly processed them with her eyes closed, and the strength of the belief sharply declined. She got rid of him, without regret and for a good reason.

This morning I spoke with Heidi before the seminar, and she told me that the distance she felt towards the relationship had grown considerably. She could see now how ridiculous the whole thing had been: The event had turned into a memory.

PARTNERSHIP
ROMANCE
BELIEFS

CELIA'S GUILT

Celia had to teach a seminar on coping with challenges. She was very nervous and didn't know how she would manage: She was a prime example of having to teach what you must learn. In a similar situation last year, she had been severely attacked by a participant. In the initial discussion, she concluded: "I'm my own greatest critic." I asked her, "from whom did this 'I' learn to criticize you? and she said: "My father."

Celia then told the story how her father always told her to do things right. One day when she was eleven years old, she had to do chores in the church for her father, who was a verger. She finished her work fast and told father she had finished. She knew her work wasn't perfect, but she wanted to play in the freshly fallen snow with her younger sister. Then an accident happened with the sleigh and her sister broke her leg, with serious consequences. Celia was made responsible. She had felt extremely guilty for the rest of her life, even though her younger sister had recently told her that she was glad that the accident had never come between them.

Two cycles of the Logosynthesis sentences followed here, one for "the wish that this hadn't happened." This eased the guilt. Then she said the sentences for a memory of being left home alone, while the parents went to the hospital with her sister. This second cycle brought enormous relief. Celia said: "I was eleven years old. I couldn't know what might happen in the fresh snow." I added a third cycle for the image of her father, which hadn't been addressed yet, and Celia was ready for the fourth sentence. In the future-pacing, she could look at her upcoming seminar with relaxed confidence: She's an experienced professional.

Guilt is always based on beliefs that you could have known or done something to prevent pain or damage. You couldn't. Children are especially susceptible to guilt, because they don't grasp the complexity of cause-effect relationships in life on earth. They tend to overestimate their own influence on human destiny. Guilt also activates experiences of deep abandonment and excludes you from feeling connected. Thus it can intensify trauma.

One of the most effective interventions is addressing these limiting beliefs with Logosynthesis. Forgiveness then becomes possible. Forgiveness is not something one does, it's the automatic result of the realization that an alternative was not available at the time.

▪
FAMILY OF ORIGIN
CHILDHOOD
ACCIDENT

BOARDING THE WRONG TRAIN

Deirdre once boarded the wrong train and had been afraid of repeating her error ever since. She was examining the history of that fear when a memory emerged: She'd once been trapped in a lift while someone was moving her piano. She couldn't breathe and thought: "I'm lost."

Another, earlier incident occurred during nursery school.

Her father had taken her to school and left without saying goodbye. The same thought of "I'm lost" had joined fear and panic. This thought of "being lost" was what lay behind her fear of boarding the wrong train. Logosynthesis helped her to dissolve the introjects – the distressing old representations of the lift, the piano and her father. Her fear then abruptly disappeared. Deirdre now pays careful attention to where she wants to go before a train leaves. She can relax prior to departure without having to get up and check the train's destination. She also remains calm during the journey.

In Deirdre's case, the scenes in the nursery school and the lift contributed to the formation of dissociative structures. The subconscious activation of these structures led to fears of things in the present. The Logosynthesis sentences release the frozen ties that bind together old memories of the outside world and challenges in the present. Deirdre can calmly think back to the old images without the memories being reactivated and panic emerging as a result.

EMOTIONS
BELIEFS
MEMORIES

WITNESSING AN EXECUTION

Peter suffered from generalized panic attacks. The first one occurred when he was 22; by the age of 28, he had found a mental strategy to control them. Now, in his fifties, they had shown up again. In a first session, we tried to identify life events which could have caused these panic reactions, but every time something seemed to come to the surface, he went blank. A careful interview, a timeline, and flash questions; no technique reached the deeper layers from which the panic attacks were being triggered.

The timeline gave at least some information: It became clear that the fear had been there for his entire life. I asked Peter if the concept of past life trauma made any sense to him. He had already wondered if something had happened to him in a past life. However, it was clear that there was no way to access traumatic memories directly. The original traumatic event at the root of the panic attacks must have been so horrible that Peter couldn't even think of it, so I changed my strategy to a more general perspective.

Bad things happen in the world, and if you read the newspapers, you're informed of them. I asked him what the worst news was he could remember reading. He didn't need much time to answer: executions, people being killed on purpose by other people. I switched to an "if, what" type of question: If an execution led to the panic attacks, what could have happened? I got a flash that the panic attacks were triggered by observing an execution, not by having been executed. Peter could identify with this idea.

In the following session, he was able to access the medieval world of a sixteen-year-old girl, witnessing the killing of her father in a riot. In the key image, an axe split the man's head. I gave Peter the Logosynthesis sentences for this image, and after the third sentence he felt himself moving away from the scene, while the girl waved at him and smiled.

After this cycle, Peter felt quiet and happy. As a future pace exercise, I asked him to leave the room, go outside and explore what was different after this session. He went out and returned after five minutes. The fear was gone. There was no reference to it in his experience outside.

Peter later shared that during the trip home he experienced a state of "just being," which continued until the following day. His body kept trembling, adapting to the new condition. He was still extremely impressed by the impact of the session.

Memory? Fantasy? Metaphor? In the practice of Logosynthesis, it doesn't matter: It's just one more energy construct to dissolve.

LIFE TRANSITIONS
TRAUMA
HEALTH AND ILLNESS

RECONNECTING WITH THE BODY

Mary is a 34-year-old marketing professional. At the age of five, she was in a car accident; hit by a drunk driver in a truck. For days, even weeks, her parents didn't know if she would survive, and they were frozen in powerless rage directed at the man who had caused their suffering. Since then, Mary had never really returned to her body. She underwent a very intense near-death experience, in which she was deeply connected with what we would call Essence, and whenever she got into conflicts with people she dissociated. She felt as if she didn't really live in her body and that her life didn't really have meaning.

In a first session, we had a long conversation about a lack of harmony between body, mind and spirit, and she felt relieved, really understood. Today I had a second session with her, and she told me that the first session had been spot on: She was not fully present. She related this to the car accident at age 5, which she referred to as "When I died." She also said, "I shouldn't have lived." She described how she had been standing in heaven and looked from above down at the site of the accident. When she came back to life, she didn't trust people anymore: "It's much more comfortable watching my life from above." She even thought that people are generally bad.

She reported that she had trusted people before the accident, so I decided to look for a perception that had let her to decide not to trust people. However, the memory of the accident was deeply buried, there were only fragments. One fragment was a squashed feeling in her right shoulder, which she experienced clearly as a memory, not as a reaction to a memory. After a round of the Logosynthesis sentences, she stretched her body. The squashed feeling had gone away. She hadn't consciously related it to the car accident: After that there had been a series of incidents in which she had hurt her shoulder.

After this round, Mary said: "I don't trust people and I don't want to be like that." On the outside everything looked fine, but internally it felt different. She also used the expression: "I don't trust myself." I pointed out to her that she must have one part called "I" that didn't trust another part called "myself." She reacted with surprise. When she started looking for the "I" part she was able to find it behind her on her right side, pushing heavily with a SUD (subjective unit of distress) score of 9 out of 10.

After she said the Logosynthesis sentences for "the part behind my back," she felt dramatically different: "Now that part is inside me, really part of me. My whole life it's been outside of my body, and I've been in a battle with myself." She felt a new strength in her solar plexus, and she looked radiant and beautiful. "This part has been in the way of my connection with Essence, and now I can start to do what I'm here for in this world, to help people. I don't like being bossed around."

Now she realized that she had had an injury on the right and that her body was balanced now. She once again started describing how she had observed the crash site, the car, the train, the police, from the clouds, with deep compassion for the drunken driver. Her parents had had a completely different attitude towards this person. They were full of anger and resentment towards him.

The emotions of the parents had led to an ambivalence for Mary, as it was very present and at the same time, she didn't share it at all. I gave her the sentences for "the parents' representation of the drunken driver" and another second sentence for "other people's representation of the drunken driver." This resulted in an even deeper relief. She told me how she had begged her mother to let go of her anger and resentment towards the man who caused the accident, and that had helped somewhat.

After these Logosynthesis sentences, she showed me the biggest smile I'd seen from her until then. The validity of the statement "I don't trust people" had dropped to a 2 out of 10. As I think there is nothing wrong with being careful, I decided to leave it there. Then she said: "I feel like my heart has opened even more." She felt her body, in her body. The split had gone. Later that day she wrote to me: "I am sooo happy. Thank you again, I feel incredible. Words cannot express my thanks. Best day ever!"

■
ACCIDENT
ESSENCE
CHILDHOOD

LIFE TRANSITIONS AND BELIEFS

We need beliefs to understand and predict what's happening in the world, and to design a strategy for our behavior. So far, so good. The problem with beliefs is that once you've installed one, it's there to stay, even though there are beliefs you'd do better without. They limit the ways you can lead your life.

This is especially the case with old beliefs, installed at ages between three and six. In this magical age, you don't have the cognitive potential to understand much of what's going on, you're surrounded by adults you depend upon for food, drink, shelter, attention and explanations, and you can't run away from home or get a second opinion. Those circumstances are ideal for the creation of simple, very limiting beliefs about yourself, others and the world.

A limiting belief can stay active as a core structure in your energy system. You grow up, your body gets stronger, your mind gets brighter, you make friends, but you don't really notice because there is a deep, strong, undifferentiated conviction that you're weak, stupid or alone. That belief will then determine your behavior. You don't exercise, you don't study, or you don't practice or do things with others. All those things don't make sense: If you *are* like that, how could you change it? In the long run, other people will start to mirror your beliefs, because you teach them through your behavior patterns.

Resolving limiting beliefs is one of the most useful applications of Logosynthesis: You don't need to reactivate early childhood experiences all the time.

WORK AND
SUCCESS

The core of any process in guided change can be summarized with two questions:

1. What are you here for in this life?
2. What keeps you from doing that?

Gerald, a 40-year-old senior consultant, told me he was here on this earth to practice being lively and to explore complexity and non-duality. To find a way beyond the polarities of good and bad, right and wrong. His three P's were Perceptions, Paradigms and Perspectives. He was experiencing difficulty at work and in achieving professional success. In his personal life, he had a hard time learning to trust people.

Another repetitive pattern of his was an ongoing internal struggle whether to take a project on himself or share the labor and the glory by working on it with others. In the process of working in the group, Gerald discovered that his concept of "work" was in fact an introject from his mother that was connected to beliefs about life, like: Work means living up to the expectations of others and involved the pressure to keep up with the Joneses, e.g., by driving a great car. From his father he had absorbed the message that it was good to do what he wanted, but when under stress mom's directives became dominant.

Then we had a discussion about the word "success." That word is very popular, and in general, success is considered as something attractive and worth striving for. Taking a closer look, however, the concept might stand in the way of your own development because people tend to depend on the positive judgment of others to feel successful.

The value and importance of both "work" and "success" depend on external criteria. They create a lot of clutter in your energy system and may distract you from your own, deeply personal mission in life.

MISSION
BELIEFS
PARENTS

DAISY'S BELIEF

Daisy is the younger of two siblings. Her brother and parents are often in conflict and share with Daisy all the gory details of their fights. Daisy feels helpless and guilty, because she feels responsible. She's not able to set boundaries with her family.

We identify the belief "I'm responsible," and the validity of the negative belief is 8-9. I guide her to find the belief in space, and she makes hand movements from which I derive she hears it in her head. After one round of the Logosynthesis sentences for the belief, the validity of the belief has gone down to a 4, and she no longer feels overwhelmed. Instead, she's annoyed: It's their conflict, not hers.

PARENTS
FAMILY OF ORIGIN
BELIEFS

REBECCA RESOLVES A BELIEF

Sixty-three-year-old Rebecca told me about her fear that her son would be imprisoned. This fear came up every time she read about a robbery, murder or rape in the newspaper. She fantasized that her 40-year-old son had committed the crimes and saw images of him behind bars in her mind's eye. She'd tried to apply Logosynthesis to this problem on several occasions, with little success.

When she introduced this topic in one of our sessions, I was able to uncover the belief behind her fear and the prison fantasy: "My son is a potential criminal."

I asked her where this belief was located in her personal space, and she replied, "Across the entire width of the room, above me." She then paused for a moment and said, "It's a guillotine … hanging over me," and began to cry. She now applied the sentences for "this guillotine hanging over me." As we went through the first cycle, the guillotine turned into an old-style parchment that was rolled up at both ends. There was a barely readable saying printed on the sheet. After the second cycle, the parchment appeared in her imagination as very old and almost falling apart. When she removed the foreign energy from the parchment with the second sentence of the third cycle, she imagined a strong sucking force pulling it far away and over the mountains.

The belief that her son was a criminal and the fear that he might commit a crime then totally disappeared.

IMAGES
BELIEFS
CHILDREN

THE CONCEPT OF LOVE

Sometimes a whole treatment involves working with a single concept. Today a client complained that she didn't feel love for her husband and children. Her saying the word "love" triggered a strange reaction in me, as if love wasn't real to her. I gave her the sentences on "this concept of love." During the working phase of the first sentence, I saw her face relaxing deeply. This relaxation process continued. After the three sentences, she said: "I feel flat, not present, not emotional." Then a situation showed up in which she had felt guilty, and we applied the sentences on the fantasy that she could have done something to prevent the misery she has been through with those she loved. She then recognized that it wasn't her fault. After another cycle about the events of the past, she said: "The sun's coming up. I feel lightness, the light of love and life. The very ones I love are around me."

■

ROMANCE
PARTNERSHIP
MEMORIES

JUDITH'S GUILT

Judith is a single mom. Separated from her long-time partner a few years ago, he now lives in another country with their son, while their seven-year-old daughter Sara lives with Judith. Sara is very rebellious, requiring much attention – you easily could call her spoiled. Judith does not refuse her anything, but that doesn't change her daughter's behavior: Sara just pushes a button and Judith runs to fulfill her every wish.

I asked Judith: "If guilt were an issue here, what would be the underlying beliefs?" She knew the answer immediately: "I'm the reason that my daughter cannot be with her father." And "I can't be available for her as much as she wants me to be."

After saying the sentences for these beliefs, Judith reported that a dark cloud was lifting. Visualizing Sara and her wishes, she said: "She can't push that button anymore. I'm responsible and I will set boundaries if necessary."

Painful separations are a part of life and of destiny, as partners, parents and children. When you decide to separate, you're doing the best you can. Even if a separation or divorce is extremely painful, staying would have hurt more. After such a separation life continues as it is, independent from what could have been done or should have been done.

These thoughts of "would" and "should" are beliefs or fantasies that lead to guilt. Reality is the only thing that counts. The guilt feelings can alienate us from those around us, and they can also keep us from taking responsibility for those we're responsible for. Judith could not own her responsibility to set parental boundaries for Sara as long as she felt guilty about the separation.

Logosynthesis helps to identify and resolve the limiting beliefs in which the guilt is rooted. Once the beliefs are resolved, all involved are able to cope with destiny.

EMOTIONS
LIFE TRANSITIONS
BELIEFS

THE
CHILD

Brenda, a graphic designer in her late thirties, became pregnant during a short affair. She knew that she didn't want to continue the relationship with the man involved, but she wasn't sure if she would be able to raise the child on her own. When she entered my practice, she was pretty certain she was going to choose to have an abortion, even though it was probably her last opportunity to become a mother.

After Brenda had told me her story and her wish to reach a decision in this session, I invited her to walk two different timelines into her future – one with and one without the child.

The future without the child was predictable: a career, money, different places and different partners. There were no blocks on this timeline; it was just a continuation of the life she had lived until now. That life seemed safe, but also a bit boring in the end.

Walking the second timeline was full of fears and blocks: a fear of childbirth, the added responsibility and financial burden of being a single mother. Each of these blocks were resolved with the help of the Logosynthesis sentences.

After returning to the here-and-now point from the two timelines Brenda discovered her decision to have the child, even though the fear wasn't completely gone. She left my office with a curious smile on her face, and I didn't hear from her until this week, when her picture showed up on a social media site, in a list of "people you may know." I sent her a message to touch base and she answered:

"I am well. It's been an interesting couple of years since we last spoke – my son is five! He is doing well. He's the apple of my eye. Motherhood could not have suited me better." Her career had developed differently from the timeline. She had lost her job due to downsizing earlier this year and after a few tough months had decided to pursue a career as a freelance designer in her field.

When I sent her a draft of this post to ask for her consent to publish it, she added an interesting detail:

"Interesting that looking back it doesn't seem like a tough decision at all! Was I leaning towards an abortion when I visited you? I know I was unsure but thought I was leaning towards keeping the child. Perhaps I remember it differently based on my decision .."

Logosynthesis is a great instrument to help someone to resolve blocks in decision-making. Decisions are made based on possible futures. Possible futures are heavily influenced by painful events from a person's past. If these blocks are moved out of the way, the decision seems like a fact that has always been part of a person's life.

LIFE TRANSITIONS
WORK
WORKING ALLIANCE

HANNAH BIDS FAREWELL

Hannah is an attractive artist in her early thirties. She's been together with Vince for quite some time. Vince is a talented, dynamic musician who leads a richly varied life and travels a lot, often taking Hannah along. Their relationship has two sides: It's full of love when the couple gets along, but Vince has a short fuse and starts to yell whenever something doesn't suit him. After a fight, he often won't talk to Hannah for two days. Hannah responds to this silence with self-loathing and grief. When Vince finally comes around, he's always quick to promise her everything under the sun.

Hannah isn't able to have a calm discussion with him about this pattern. Vince has made a half-hearted attempt to address the issue with a therapist, but this ended without success. Hannah turned to me for help to figure out what to do. When we started to talk it was clear that she was in despair about the relationship. A short while ago she'd been convinced that Vince was the man for her and that he'd change if only she loved him enough. She wanted to give the love another chance, but she didn't really believe that anything would change.

The process of the session highlighted many elements of the grieving process: Hannah was in despair because Vince hadn't kept his promise and she had to give up the belief that he'd change. Logosynthesis had to be applied to this belief.

Rage emerged once this cycle was complete. He had lied to her repeatedly and manipulated her. The rage was a reaction to the words of his promises and his faithful expression. After the application of Logosynthesis she had become aware that he had not kept his promises – and never would.

Now a fantasy appeared – that Vince would soon have new girlfriends if she would break up with him. This fantasy intensified her grief. She received the sentences for the fantasy, and her grief became even more intense. It seemed as if she was now facing the reality of the loss.

Hannah realized that she would not only lose the relationship with Vince, but also the music scene that filled her shared life with him. That tie would also be severed in a breakup. She processed the images of this scene with the sentences.

We then addressed her fantasy of an ideal relationship with Vince. The energy that was bound up in this fantasy was also taken back. Hannah cried for several minutes. The grieving process was really under way.

The belief now emerged that a new boyfriend necessarily had to be a boring boyfriend. Hannah took her energy from this fantasy as well.

When our session came to an end, Hannah reported that she felt better and more relaxed. She said soberly: "It's not going to work with Vince."

EMOTIONS
WISHES AND DESIRES
FANTASIES

THE WORLD AS I WANT IT

Serena is a lively 35-year-old who lives with her husband and 12-year-old daughter. She manages a small team in a health care setting. Recently, an interpersonal conflict with one of her team members resulted in his leaving the team. Serena felt depressed and disappointed, especially having invested much time and energy trying to solve this personality conflict with her team member.

This was only one in a series of problems, which could all be distilled to one central theme: Life isn't perfect. Life is not as I want it to be. Until now, she has tried to meet challenges by studying to understand and learn more: more theory, more methods, a master's diploma, but this time that strategy didn't seem to work. I felt compassion for her, but realized that learning more was not going to provide the solution to this woman at this stage of her life.

The problem was that she couldn't accept life as it is as a woman in her thirties with a significant responsibility in an organization. You can be optimistic, but life won't fulfill all your desires. You can try hard, you can try to be perfect, you can try to please everybody, but there will always be a team member or a boss who shows you that there are limits.

Serena hadn't really discovered those practical limits before in her life. Her training had prepared her well for the content and context of her work, but not for the blocks life itself put on her path. When she was challenged in the professional arena, her strategy had been to acquire more training and supervision, but it never seemed enough to meet all the demands in her daily life. She always wanted to "make it better" and took sole responsibility for everything that went wrong or anyone who felt bad in the workplace.

Serena's key issue is the inability to transition from a stage in life in which she developed by learning from others, in a safe learning environment, to a stage in which she has to learn to carry responsibility, without relying on other experts. She was the expert now, in a team that wasn't perfect, in an organization that wasn't perfect, in a world that wasn't perfect. Such a transition is not a problem to be solved. It requires a transformation.

Serena was familiar with Logosynthesis. She had tried to apply it on the surface level, with the images of her annoying colleague and her boss. That hadn't worked, which wasn't surprising. She hadn't recognized the deeper level of the issue: She had wanted to create an ideal world. I gave her as a first sentence:

"I retrieve all my energy, bound up in the world as I want it to be, and take it to the right place in my Self."

After repeating that sentence, she started to cry. A few minutes passed. Then she started to relax and smile through her tears, and I offered her the second sentence, which didn't show much visible effect. I gave her the third sentence in the lost fantasy form:

"I retrieve all my energy, bound up in all my reactions to *the fact that this world as I want it to be does not exist,* and take it to the right place in my Self, in the here-and-now as an adult woman."

Again tears welled for a moment, but the work had been done. She looked at me with clear eyes and said, in a firm, deep voice: "Maybe there is another way I haven't considered yet."

Training situations often tend to create an illusory frame of mind in which there seems to be a satisfying solution for every problem. In reality there isn't. This can be a trap for trainees as well as trainers: trying to create a world in which everything is OK.

■
WORK
WISHES AND DESIRES
LIFE TRANSITIONS

EXPLORING THE VOID

Emily, a 30-year-old consultant, came to see me because she wasn't satisfied with the direction her life had taken. She still received financial support from her parents, who were very involved in her life and had strong opinions on what she should and shouldn't do. In fact, her whole life was crowded with people who determined her actions. When I asked her, in a repetitive way, who she was and what she wanted, she only expressed very general wishes for happiness and meaning. None of these vague sentiments would ever be able to compete with the requirements from her parents.

In my own countertransference, I noticed irritation: I didn't have any trouble identifying with her parents, but that wasn't helpful. Emily answered every question within a fraction of a second with: "I don't know." It seemed to be forbidden to think, to have an opinion, to have a personal goal. There was no space for her own, unique Self.

To explore this, I asked her to imagine an empty space around her. When she tried this, she panicked, the void was too confronting. I took her to an empty place in the room, let her find a position for herself and then let her find out how big her personal space was. It was only as large as her body. When I asked her to widen the boundaries of her space, she started moving around in growing circles, visibly relaxed, until I let her return to the center of her circle. Now she felt the newly discovered space shrinking again to the size of her body, and she looked at me with fiery eyes.

No Logosynthesis sentences today. I couldn't find a way to slice this massive pattern into slices that could be processed. There was so much more to do before she would be able to feel safe with me. Safe enough to explore her personal space, the void from which to hear Essence calling.

In the next session, Emily had taken a break, and the effect was amazing. She had realized that she needed to expand her space and that there were parental messages that kept her from discovering what she really wanted in life. She had also become aware that she needed confirmation and permission at every step, which was debilitating with parental messages telling her to be different.

Emily's fearful gaze was now gone, and her eye contact with me was clear. She was able to explore the content of her patterns instead of dissociating immediately. I let her make a list of those messages and decide which was the most limiting. This time was the right time for the Logosynthesis sentences. One message was "Why are you always like this?" connected to the conclusion "I'm weird." This and a few other messages could now easily be neutralized with the sentences. Emily started to discover a world of her own, not determined by the wishes, values, ideas and commands of others. Her energy changed completely; in the team an open exchange about different options available to her became possible.

■
MISSION
LIFE TRANSITIONS
FAMILY OF ORIGIN

THE PAIN BEHIND THE BIG PICTURE

Brian complained that he couldn't remember details of his own life story, it was like watching a blank canvas when he became introspective about his life. An intelligent man, he was good at analysis and abstract thought, but felt unnerved by his inability to recall his own experience. His own history was a mystery, his only memory was being in his parents' bedroom, alone in a panic.

Suspecting this wasn't a medical condition, I shared with him my hypothesis that he had blanked out his life's history as a self-protection mechanism. The lack of personal memories was the manifestation of a second order dissociation, adopted as protection against the pain of first order dissociation

– abandonment. As he listened to this theory about why he couldn't remember his own life, vague early memories began to surface.

When we processed these early memories with Logosynthesis sentences, he reacted with strong physical sensations. Each time, the distress was greatly diminished, and new memories and traumatic events associated with shame and loneliness surfaced and were processed. At the end of the session, Brian said, "This is going to change my life." I shared that I expected more repressed memories would surface, now that his subconscious mind has learned that these could be processed. Brian didn't need to build a wall against his own mind anymore to protect himself against the deepest pain of abandonment.

FAMILY OF ORIGIN
MEMORIES
WORKING ALLIANCE

OLIVER'S TESTS AT SCHOOL

Oliver is 15. Growing fast, he is a bright high school student, with clear friendly eyes and an interested gaze, the young intellectual type.

He comes in with his mother, who describes an interesting but disturbing symptom: When Oliver has a test in school he forgets everything he has learned as soon as he sees the test paper with the questions.

I remember that in our first session three years ago Oliver was a good ally in the process, so I engage him in a conversation as if he were a psychologist colleague. Drawing a diagram on the flip chart in my consulting room, I ask, "What's the matter in this mysterious case? We have a bright young guy as a client, who suddenly is unable to perform."

What happens in the process? He studies for the test, knows everything covered, he receives the test questions, looks over the sheet to get an overview of the exam, and when he begins to answer, he has forgotten everything he learned. Mysterious, indeed. Oliver's reaction when he realizes that he can't pass the test is "sh*t."

I draw a formula on the flip chart, with a sheet of paper on the left, an F for forgetting in the middle, and "sh*t" on the right. In our psychological conversation, we try to find out if there is any additional information, but we can't find anything, so I draw a black box between the sheet of paper and the F for forgetting. I tell Oliver that, in my opinion, the "sh*t" is not relevant: Once he stops forgetting, there will no longer be a reason to be irritated.

So we concentrate on the black box. Oliver is fascinated by the way I take this problem apart and he tries to help me where he can. I come up with the idea that there must be a stress reaction. Something happens, which causes his brain to switch to a state of "empty." I'm really puzzled and look at my colleague helplessly: What, for heaven's sake, is in that black box?

Psychologist Oliver finally comes up with the answer himself: "I put myself under pressure." I notice that that's a very interesting statement, because it means that he has two parts: One part is called "I." That part exerts pressure on the other part that's called "myself." Oliver is confused by the idea of being split in two parts, so I explain the top dog-underdog mechanism in the black box.

The I-part of Oliver gives a strong message to the myself-part that he is not allowed to fail the test. The myself-part reacts to this message with a stress reaction, turning off the part of his brain that can access what he has studied. It instead goes into a state of alarm, and he freezes. Now Oliver gets it: The I-part gives the orders, the myself-part must comply, but the myself-part is scared of the I-part and panics.

I ask Oliver where the two parts are in the room, and he discovers that they share the same space in the middle of his head. I conclude that it's too confusing to keep them in the same spot. I invite him to find a place for the I-part and the myself-part on my carpet, and then a third spot for the Oliver that doesn't have the problem. These spots are marked with colored paper disks.

Once the map is laid out, I ask Oliver where the most energy is bound from his position of Oliver who doesn't have the problem. It's the I-part marker that he feels pushed by. Now I give him the Logosynthesis sentences for that I-part. They take a long time to process, especially the second one, which is not surprising. When I ask what happened to the I-part, he says, amazed: "Both parts have become much weaker."

Oliver is pleasantly surprised. His back has straightened, his eyes shine even more brightly, and when we go through the formula on the flip chart again, the I-part is taken out of the equation. That means that the myself-part also disappears and that we can leave the answers to the test questions to this healthy, intelligent 15-year-old.

Two weeks later:

> *Good Afternoon Dr. Lammers:*
>
> *We were with you two weeks ago. On Friday I had my mathematics exam and the result was a B+. I almost wrote an A-flat! The sentences have helped me to get my nervousness completely under control, and since then I am getting good grades again. Thank you for your help!*
>
> *Greetings and Thanks,*
>
> *Oliver*

WORKING ALLIANCE
WORK
EMOTIONS

FAMILY OF ORIGIN

When your own personal space gets bigger, it will necessarily interfere with those of others, and it's not surprising that long hidden conflicts show up on the surface of your awareness. You realize that this is not how you want the world to be. All the time you have held back your needs, you were not even aware of them. Now you are aware, not only of your needs and desires in the here-and-now, but also of all those that were unfulfilled in the past.

This is confusing for you, and the reactions you get can push you back into the old familiar fear. However, if you examine this process thoroughly, you learn to recognize which needs and wishes can be fulfilled by those around you, and which needs you must give up.

You must learn to accept that you didn't, don't and won't have ideal parents, siblings teachers and bosses, and that your spouse, your friends or your colleagues are not here to compensate for those deficits. In this process, anger and grief are closely connected. You have to give up fantasies about the world and its people: about how they should be, could be, should have been or could have been.

LOSING MONEY, BECOMING POOR

Liz had a fear of losing all her money and becoming poor. She is married and approaching retirement. She and her husband ran a consulting business together and now they want to create a new common space. It became immediately evident that there was no rational reason for this fear of poverty. Liz was aware of this herself, but this didn't stop her from being afraid.

When we continued to explore what the fear was about, she told me that she was afraid to lose her house and have to live in a one-room apartment, under a bridge, or worse. She feared a loss of dignity. When I asked her what was the worst that could happen if she lost her dignity, she answered: "Loneliness." She touched on a very deep pain, with roots in her personal history.

I asked for those roots, and she came up with two images. In the first one, she was three or four years old, sitting in the kitchen, watching and listening to her parents discussing the financial concerns of the family. The child understood that they were sad and upset; she wanted to help but she was desperate and lonely because as a child she didn't understand.

In the other memory Liz was somewhat younger, on a walk with her parents. She fell behind, and even though she ran as fast as she could on her shaky little legs, she could not catch up. Her mother looked at her from a distance and seemed amused. She was afraid her parents would leave her behind.

I asked Liz in which image most energy was bound; she didn't know. In such a situation, I usually start with the earliest situation. Later memories tend to be neutralized by resolving the earlier material. The first memory had a strong visual component: the image of her parents walking away from her. She said the Logosynthesis sentences for this image, and it lost its significance immediately. She could recognize that her parents had been gently challenging her.

The second image remained active. She felt desperate and alone being unable to help her parents. When I gave her the sentences for this memory, already the first sentence had an immediate effect. The second sentence took a long time to process and gave further deeper relief. After the third sentence, Liz started to laugh. The fear of losing money? It was gone. It had not been her own, but her parents' fear.

PARENTS
MEMORIES
EMOTIONS

DRIVING

Lonnie had a phobia around driving a car, and riding for long distances in a car with her husband caused her to panic. She said, "I feel trapped" and the thought that there was no farm or other building for miles around made her feel anxious. When I went back in time with her to the origin of the anxiety, it had been there all her life, even at birth.

When I guided Lonnie through the time before her birth, the fear was not there during the first three months in the womb. What had happened? She told a story of a car accident her parents were involved in. It was in the fourth month of Lonnie's time in the womb. The car was totaled. Nobody was really hurt, though her mother had gone into shock.

When we did the Logosynthesis sentences on behalf of Lonnie's mother, there was an enormous relief, with deep sighs, in particular after the second sentence. On returning to the memory of the womb, Lonnie switched immediately to her birth, and said, "I'm trapped!" These were the exact words she had used to describe her experience in the car. At the time of birth, she had been actually trapped, because her delivery had taken more than 24 hours due to a breech presentation.

When we did the sentences for Lonnie's perception of the body of her mother at birth, there was again a deep relief. When I asked her to visualize the upcoming long journey in the car, she started to smile and said: "I'm looking forward to our holidays!"

PARENTS
ACCIDENT
EMOTIONS

THE VIRTUAL TWIN

Claire was working through a life theme when the image of a little child appeared. Usually this represents a split-off part of the client, and applying the sentences leads to the dissolution of such an image. This time it didn't. The child turned its back to Claire and walked away a few steps. I was puzzled. In the reassessment stage after the sentences, Claire told me that her grandmother had died after having given birth to stillborn twin boys.

I decided to give Claire the sentences for the representation of those twins. After the second sentence, Claire experienced a long-held tension moving out of her body. The image of the twins changed into two gray spots, completely disappearing after a second round of the sentences.

When Claire returned to the image of the child in her

personal space, she saw the child walking away, and felt incredible relief. The traumatic death of her grandmother after the birth of twins had led to the energy construct of a twin sibling when Claire's mother became pregnant.

IMAGES
TRAUMA
FAMILY OF ORIGIN

I'M NOT GOOD ENOUGH

Monica, 39, has a three-year-old son and works as a coach in the Human Resources department of a large company. She's recently become aware of a lifelong belief: "I'm not good enough." and discovered through a series of flash questions that the belief had been there from birth.

Her birth was accelerated because her father, a flight engineer, had to leave the family for an extended time. In accessing the birth experience, she realized she hadn't wanted to be born yet. Something was missing: She wanted to wait for her twin brother – recently Monica's mother had revealed to her that she had not been alone in the womb.

She did the sentences for the unfulfilled wish to have her brother join her. After that, she felt better about entering the world alone. Her attitude shifted to "OK, let's give it a go." I gave her the sentences for "the energy of the body of my mother," a procedure I often use to process birth experiences at a deep level. Then I checked with Monica about the belief of not being good enough, and she said: "It's good now."

I now asked Monica to think of her childhood. A Christmas memory showed up, of herself as a four-year-old. Her dearest wish had been to receive a baby doll as a present, with eyes that close when it's laid down. Instead, her mom fulfilled her own dearest wish; a beautiful, very expensive doll with a porcelain head, and painted eyes. A picture of that evening showed how Monica was appalled and how her mother had been beaming with joy.

We did the Logosynthesis sentences for the doll and everything it represented. After the first sentence, Monica felt a deep rage and saw herself throwing the doll around the room. We did another cycle for the wishes of her mother. After this the rage faded, and for the first time her father showed up. As an engineer, he was rarely home, and when he was home, he stayed out of the conflicts between his wife and Monica. She realized she had believed she was not good enough because he hadn't protected her from her mother's angry attacks. In the simple logic of the child: If she had been good enough, her father would have protected her.

We did a last cycle for the unfulfilled wish that her father had protected her. Then she said dryly: "He had his own issues." I asked, "What about the belief that you're not good enough?" Monica replied, with a big smile: "That's resolved."

BELIEFS
IMAGES
FAMILY OF ORIGIN

HER PLACE
IN THE SUN

In the Logosynthesis Live seminar, Susie made a map of her family situation when she was three. Her father was absent traveling, and her mother as well as her nanny were preoccupied with their own newly born babies. She felt extremely lonely, her place in the sun taken over by her new sister and the nanny's baby.

In the treatment process, she went through the positions of the adults involved, one after the other, and discovered how much each of them had suffered their own way. Father had lost his mother as a young boy and had transferred his love for his deceased mother to his daughter, excluding his wife, and inadvertently made a mother figure out of his daughter. Mother felt abandoned by her husband because of this. After applying Logosynthesis on these issues of the parental introjects, the client felt utter relief.

The icing on the cake: Immediately after we finished, her phone rang. She was annoyed, because she always carefully switched it off. When she looked at the display, she couldn't believe her eyes. Her younger sister, who hadn't called her in 20 years, had just called her from Hong Kong.

FAMILY OF ORIGIN
CHILDHOOD
SOCIOENERGETIC FIELDS

GIVEN AWAY

Judy's parents couldn't take care of her. Immediately after her birth they placed her in a very loving foster family. She bounced around in foster families and homes until she turned 18. To handle this tumultuous upbringing, she developed the coping pattern of being cute and striving towards perfection, to avoid rejection. She managed her circumstances as well as she could and has grown up into a successful adult. Now she's getting older and feels driven by these patterns formed in her childhood, hounded by a persistent sense of not living her life. I offered that trying to be perfect and pleasing to others could have been her way of preventing herself from being abandoned. She had never thought of this. She had been aware of her perfectionism, but not of the reason behind it.

Judy was invited to find three places in space for the moment of separation from her parents: one for herself, one for her mother, and one for her father. When she took the place of herself as a baby just born, she was overwhelmed by pain and grief. She then stood on the place of her mother and became her mother. The mother was also overwhelmed by grief and guilt. I gave her the Logosynthesis sentences – as her mother – to retrieve her own energy from her daughter and to give her daughter's energy back. The tension reduced, but the grief wasn't fully resolved. Then she said the sentences for the wish that her daughter could have stayed with her. Now, as the mother, she relaxed, and took her own place again. The pain of the newborn was now greatly diminished.

She repeated this same procedure from the position of her father, and after that she said, back on the place of herself as a baby: "This is my destiny, I can't change it, and it's OK." Back in her seat as an adult woman, she couldn't feel the perfectionist attitude that had been her strategy to cope with the current challenges in her life. She said, "I'm doing the best I can. That's good enough for me and for other people."

The abandonment of the first order dissociation was covered up by the drive to be cute and perfect. This second order dissociation had led to a feeling of alienation: a nice, perfect robot. Addressing the original separation trauma made the need for the perfectionistic coping behavior redundant.

CHILDHOOD
FAMILY OF ORIGIN
EMOTIONS

SHE SHOULD HAVE BEEN A BOY

Joan had recently experienced a conflict with her boss. When I asked if her own behavior reminded her of someone else in her history, she recalled a memory of her music teacher when she was nine. She then jumped further back in her history to her mother, who had been confrontational and aggressive, while her father was a very soft, tolerant man. Then suddenly, a memory surfaced; her grandmother had always said that she should have been a boy.

I let her map the situation around her birth. Her grandmother, her mother, and her father were placed in positions. Where she felt most tension was in the place representing grandmother. I let her take this position, become her grandmother, and interviewed her in this role. As grandmother she declared that she was proud of her granddaughter, but "she should have been a boy." I had her turn towards the client's position and say the Logosynthesis sentences on this belief. Grandmother felt some relief, but the process wasn't fully resolved. In the next step, I had her say the sentences for the unfulfilled wish that she had wanted the client to be a boy. This fully resolved the introject: As her grandmother, Joan visibly relaxed.

When she returned to her own place in the map, the tension she had felt towards her grandmother had disappeared. Now the energy bound up in the relationship with her mother came to the foreground. The next steps repeated those in the work with the grandmother introject: Her mother had also wanted her to be a boy. After she had said the same sentences from the position of her mother, she was deeply relaxed.

Once she returned to her own position as the baby just born, the metamorphosis was amazing. Her voice had become stronger, and she stood tall and straight. When I asked her to visualize the scene with her boss, she noticed that her attitude had changed from defensive to cooperative. A confrontation no longer felt necessary.

■
WISHES AND DESIRES
FAMILY OF ORIGIN
WORK

THE GIRL WITH THE MATCHES

Irene regularly got into trouble because she was always trying to help people. She would anticipate the needs of her boss, but she never made a clear contract about her role, so this led to unnecessary misunderstandings and interpersonal conflicts. When I started exploring this pattern with her, she told the story of her parents' divorce when she was three. Her mother was completely overwhelmed when her husband left and told Irene that she was the only one she could rely on. Mother stayed in that victim position, and Irene assumed responsibility without asking.

Irene was also a victim of the situation. In those early days, she lost her father and grandfather through the divorce, and from her mother she couldn't expect parental care. In a naive, desperate attempt to prevent her mom from becoming unhinged, Irene became a "parentified child." She started protecting her mother against everything that could possibly upset her, as if she were her own child, and this became the template for her role in society. Because this was the magical solution of a little girl, Irene never learned to negotiate or make a contract with her boss when something needed to be done: She took responsibility before anything could happen.

This smart solution of little Irene ended her childhood. Her belief was that her needs could only be met at the cost of taking care of others. I asked what would happen if she stopped caring for others. She pictured Hans Christian Andersen's story of the girl with the matches; she didn't belong to a family and died outside in the cold. She became very sad when she contemplated this, and I gave her the Logosynthesis sentences for "the mother I never had." After the third sentence, she wept. Then I gave her the sentences for "the girl with the matches."

After the cycle she murmured: "This is a sad story, but it's not about me." After this, we discussed how she could negotiate with her mother about her priorities. In a few months, she's going to be a mother herself, and that means that she won't be able to take care of her mother in the same way.

Taking the role of the parentified child was Irene's way out of the trauma of the parents' separation. The underlying abandonment was not directly accessible, but it was represented in the metaphor of the girl with the matches.

PARENTS
FAMILY OF ORIGIN
CHILDHOOD

I DON'T KNOW MY BOUNDARIES

Patty regularly overextended herself past her physical boundaries. She said this with a light, somewhat rebellious smile and added that she ignored the advice of others who told her she should do less. In our discussion I pointed out to her that there was a part that ignored her bodily needs and a part that set the boundaries the first part ignored. She was puzzled by this interpretation, and she became curious.

When I asked what caused her to transgress her own boundaries, she said: "I'll show them!" "Show what?" I asked. "That I can do it." The fact that she must prove to other people that she could do it led me to the conclusion that there was another part, which didn't seem capable. I checked this with her, and she confirmed that, and even more: That part felt worthless. Now she was visibly moved by this awareness. She hadn't realized that she was suppressing something.

When asked what made this part feel worthless, Patty's face darkened: It had started when she wasn't the youngest child in the family anymore, and Mom's affection had turned towards her younger siblings. When she lost her mother's full attention, she had concluded that she wasn't worth her mother's focus. Then she had started to prove that she was also there. I asked for a memory, and she told me how she saw herself sitting apart from the rest of the family, while her parents took care of the little children.

I gave her the Logosynthesis sentences for this image, and after that she said, with a completely different, adult tone of voice: "Mom made the right decision in giving the younger ones more attention. They needed it."

The "worthless" part had dissolved after this cycle. The "I'll show them" part also lost its strength. When I asked Patty to imagine how she would manage her physical boundaries now, she described how she could listen to the signals of her body and take a rest when needed.

CHILDHOOD
PARENTS
IMAGES

SHOWING YOUR SELF

Cindy gets a new job. She's young, bright, professional, highly motivated and she gets the job done. Her boss decides that she has potential and promotes her to a position which involves presentations, and suddenly she panics. She just can't do it.

Let's explore what happened. It starts at an early age. Cindy's mother is a needy, insecure woman, who has difficulty accepting her daughter's growing independence from her. Whenever Cindy showed signs of independence, her mother got scared and reacted by withdrawing from her, suddenly becoming cynical and aloof – the way her own mother had treated her. As soon as her mother withdrew, Cindy suddenly felt alone and became scared in turn.

Cindy learned very fast how to protect her mother from being scared and herself from being rejected, albeit at a high price. She noticed that her mother relaxed if she worked hard at school and if she took care of other people, without showing that she had her own wishes or ideas. She practiced this way of being for twenty years. It was Cindy's way of being accepted, and it helped her through school, helped her pass her exams and get a job pretty easily.

The structure of her first job matched with what she had learned: "Work hard and please people!" Therefore it's not surprising that her boss was satisfied with her performance. In the new job he offered Cindy, she was asked to come out of hiding and to show her real Self. However, the expression of this Self had always been punished by the withdrawal of her mother's love and attention. Her mother couldn't support the development of Cindy's real Self, because she never learned to express her own.

If you look at Cindy's problem from a surface level, her reaction to the new job is surprising. It could not be expected from what she's shown in the workplace before. A coaching process would probably start with encouragement, emphasizing her potential with the usual "Yes You Can," phrases or try to train her presentation skills. Would it work? Probably not. Creating a new positive introject to compete with an old negative one is rarely successful: The old one has twenty years of experience in effectively running the client's limbic system.

On a deeper level, Cindy's reaction is understandable. The Logosynthesis treatment strategy is simple: Identify the introject, locate it and neutralize it. In this case Cindy may first need a longer interview, in which the professional can offer an interpretation about why she reacts this way. Once Cindy realizes her aversion to presenting comes from avoiding to activate the loneliness and fear of a mother introject, she will be able to resolve this mother energy structure with the help of the Logosynthesis sentences.

As a result, Cindy will be able to express her real Self, and eventually, as part of this process, can take a course in public speaking. Her boss will be satisfied with her and his decision.

CHILDHOOD
PARENTS
LIFE TRANSITIONS

PHYSICAL ABUSE

Transgressions of the boundaries of the body are among the most traumatic experiences people can have, especially if the person experiencing it is of a young age and if the perpetrator should have protected and supported them.

A trauma is something that goes beyond the normal experience of a human being, and that means it cannot be processed in the higher centers of the brain. The memory is frozen at the level of the amygdala in the limbic system. The components of the frozen memory complex can be addressed and resolved with Logosynthesis as soon they emerge in a session, without the necessity of any interpretation.

For this work, the client must trust the professional and the method, and this trust is usually built up in the context of ongoing psychotherapy focusing on other issues. The abuse will emerge as soon as the client feels safe: The subconscious mind doesn't need to suppress problems that can be solved.

STRANGLED BY GRANDFATHER

Ava, a counselor, was having difficulty concluding her sessions. Often when the time was almost up, a client suddenly presented a completely new issue. She was thrown off-guard, not knowing how to end that session without cutting off the client abruptly. As a result of engaging with the client on this last-minute revelation, she often went overtime of her session length. As her workday progressed and she fell further behind schedule, her stress increased.

In the initial interview, it became clear that she expected a client to stay with the problem first presented. We discussed the nature of counseling: New issues will show up in every process, and this is to be expected. I gave her the Logosynthesis sentences for "the fantasy of 'ideal' clients who stay with their initial issue."

After this cycle she laughed about the unrealistic expectation she had for her clients to stay on task. Then a new, deeper issue showed up unexpectedly (much like the last-minute revelations of her clients at the end of their sessions). Ava described a pressure around her throat and shared that her grandfather had regularly strangled her as a small child. The resolution was relatively straightforward; Logosynthesis sentences for "the hands of grandfather strangling me" produced a state of deep relaxation.

Cycling back to re-evaluate and discuss the initial issue, Ava had reframed her initial problem with going overtime in her sessions. She now realized that her difficulty wasn't an inability to set limits, but a lack of professional experience; she didn't yet know how to conclude a therapy session with professional finesse.

Proactively educating herself by engaging in discussions with experienced counselors, she received a number of suggestions she was easily able to understand and implement.

▪
FAMILY OF ORIGIN
TRAUMA
WORK

THE HANDS OF
MY FATHER

Chrissie's stress level considerably increased on the first day of the seminar, along with tinnitus symptoms. On the second day, she realized that this anxiety was activated by my hands. The shape of my hands was similar to those of her father's, and he had worn almost the same ring. He had hit her with those hands.

When she told the story in the group, I stretched out my right hand towards her at a distance of one meter and asked her for the level of distress on a 0–10 scale. It was a 10.

I invited her to say the Logosynthesis sentences for "the hands of Willem and everything they represent" which she did. After the cycle, I stretched out my hand again, and asked for the level of distress. There was no distress left, and she shook my hand.

Another participant in the group noticed that I hadn't addressed her father's hands directly. I asked Chrissie to concentrate on an image of her father's hands, and this caused no distress for her. The subconscious mind is our faithful servant in this work.

PARENTS
FAMILY OF ORIGIN
CHILDHOOD

FREEDOM
FROM SLAVERY

Fatima's story is unbelievable. Growing up in the countryside in North Africa, her father was poisoned by a jealous aunt when she was three. Then, as a four-year-old, her mother sold her to a family in the capital. She had to work from dawn to dusk, often without food, and was regularly beaten by her mistress, at times with an iron chain. She slept on the hard floor in the hall of the house. She saw her mother only every two years when she came to collect the money for the slavery contract.

Once, during one of those visits Fatima told her mother how she was treated and begged her to take her home. When Fatima's mother discussed her story with the mistress, the woman got very angry and accused Fatima of being a liar. The mistress then blackmailed Fatima into staying, threatening her that something terrible would happen to her little sister if she left. After this incident, Mother left again for two years, after which she was sold to another family.

After our first phone call, before our session, Fatima writes me a long letter, in which she describes the child slavery, the forced marriage at the age of fifteen. She recounts the rage of her mother-in-law, who didn't want her son to be married to a slave and tried to poison her. Instead, her three-year-old son drank the poison and died in Fatima's arms. Another child died at four under mysterious circumstances.

Many years later, her then husband went to Switzerland to work and she was to follow him. Somehow she managed to free herself from the marriage to marry a Swiss man.

Minute Miracles **87**

She is very happy with him, but she's haunted by the traumatic past. In the evening she feels herself leaving her body, panic attacks follow in which she re-experiences the horrible past.

Murder, torture, rape – nothing is left out in Fatima's destiny. In the hall of the building I meet a slender, elegantly dressed woman. She's beautiful. Strangely, there is nothing in her presentation that suggests the story she has shared with me. She must be enormously strong to live through all that and then manage to look like this. Her German has only a light accent, when she arrived in Switzerland she learned it within months with the help of friends.

In my consulting room, I decide to leave the lead to her. I tell her I don't need to hear more of the story. She has written enough to show me that she has an amazing memory, which is also very precise in the description of the events. That allows us to address specific aspects of the trauma, so I'm hopeful, even though I have a deep respect for the suffering that has come with her destiny. It's my task to provide a solid frame within which she can fully arrive in the here-and-now. I propose that we address one or two issues to find out if the Logosynthesis methods will work with her. She fully agrees with that strategy and immediately mentions two incidents she wants to process.

The first one is the visit of her mother in the capital. When she went to sleep after that visit, she had the experience of dying. Her body grew cold from her feet up, and when the cold sensation had reached her head, she lost consciousness. When she came to her senses, she was deeply disappointed to be still alive – she had asked God to take her away from this earth.

We activate the scene and address it with the sentences. I propose saying the sentences on her behalf, but she insists on repeating them herself. She goes into deep reprocessing, and I let her repeat each sentence a few times. After this first round she has gone from despair to rage at her mother who had sold her to this mistress. I let her say the sentences for the image of her mother to which she reacts with that rage.

Now there is a deep relief. A broad, happy smile appears on her face. This is what she has come for and she knows it. She says that there is still something there in the scene. She sees the houses in the neighborhood near the palace in the capital. I have her say the Logosynthesis sentences for that image, and the result is moving: She sees the palace turn into a home for children who have been freed from slavery. In her letter she had written to me that this is what she considers her life mission.

The issue she brings up now is even more disturbing. She describes her three-year-old son dying in her arms after drinking the poison her mother-in-law concocted for her.

Fatima's grief and guilt are immense, unbearable. Her little sunshine died in her place. I hold the space now and give her the Logosynthesis sentences. She repeats them in tears. I let her say the sentences several times, confirming through my clear, commanding voice that I'm there with her. A part of Fatima has died in that moment; it's lying in a grave with the cold body of her little son. He was the first person who loved her; he was her sunshine.

We move on with the sentences, through the scene in the grave, and then we discuss where her son is now. We agree that he must have gone to another, better place, and I offer her a sentence in which she sends her son's energy to where he needs it now. Then there is a long silence and a deep peace. It is as if a divine light enters the room. Tears of love, of freedom, of joy are in her eyes.

MISSION
CHILDREN
FAMILY OF ORIGIN

STAYING IN BED ALL DAY

Maggie was frozen in a state of passivity, staying in bed all day, and avoiding work deadlines. If you're self-employed, such a pattern is going to cause problems sooner or later, and she was aware of that. On the surface, the issue was her passivity and a driving voice that told Maggie to go to work. On a level deeper, self-doubts showed up, such as a belief that "I can't trust myself." I pointed out that this sentence contained a strong part, "I" that had to support a vulnerable part "myself" and I asked her to explore that vulnerable part. I didn't want to focus on the strong part, because this part would become redundant if the energy bound up in the vulnerable part were reconnected to Essence.

Maggie was invited to access the vulnerable part and with what age it was associated. At first, she went blank. Then there was a connection to the age of seven and the word "exhausting" came to mind. She went one step further back in time and saw an image of herself. She was sitting on the floor in her room as a two-year-old, feeling extremely lonely, in the presence of a male. She did not know who he was or what was going on. She said the sentences for "the presence of the man behind me" and as a result she could access more layers of the memory. She felt a threat now. I counted to three and suggested that at three there would be additional information available, about the nature of the threat. This worked.

At the count of three, Maggie realized with a shock that it was her father who was the threat. He pressed her against him, and I let her say the Logosynthesis sentences for "the frozen perception of his body." After the first sentence, she felt a strong tension in her jaw, after the second she got cold, and after the third, she was extremely shaken. She had been aware of the abuse, but she had never known before that it had been her father, and now she knew – for sure. The memory deeply buried had finally surfaced.

Maggie said the sentences for "the father I had wished for and never had' and an immense grief welled up in her. Then she said matter-of-factly: "This is not simple, but now it's clear." In the next steps, she resolved with the sentences different aspects of the sexual abuse that had followed. Each time I counted to three to reveal and activate the next frame of the traumatic memory, which was then resolved using the sentences.

This had been the first in a series of extreme boundary transgressions, and it was amazing how fast it could be released. When I guided her back to the here-and-now, asking her to imagine a morning in bed, she saw herself waking up and dressing to go out. In her imagination, there was not a trace of the recent passivity.

WORKING ALLIANCE
SEXUAL ABUSE
MEMORIES

THE FROZEN THREE-YEAR-OLD

Sally strongly identified with a part of herself as a three-year-old, which had split off in the aftermath of childhood sexual abuse. When I gave her sentence 1 to integrate that frozen part, she became very scared, because she had a fantasy that she would disappear. This made perfect sense. If you identify with a child part, it cannot be integrated without losing the "I" of that part.

In Logosynthesis terms, the part – the frozen state – consists of linked energy structures of perceptions and reactions. She was only aware of her emotions (i.e. reactions), apart from the sensation of a heavy weight on her body. The perceptions were hidden from her consciousness.

I reflected upon this and found a way to treat the frozen state of her three-year-old self from another perspective: If there has been abuse, there exist frozen perceptions from all five senses. Since she wasn't consciously aware of any perceptions, apart from the heavy weight, I decided to address frozen smells, with the sentence: "I retrieve all my energy bound in the frozen perception of smells in that disturbing situation." After the first sentence, she told me, quietly, that she couldn't perceive any smells.

When she repeated the sentence a second time, she said in the same rational way that there were three potentially relevant smells: alcohol, semen and vomit. I asked her for the most important and she said: "alcohol." I let her repeat the sentence for the frozen perception of alcohol, and she realized that she and her family had always been in danger when alcohol was involved. This had continued in her adult life with her family. She said the sentences for that belief and immediately felt relieved. The panic around alcohol disappeared.

If a memory is hidden, you can give the sentences for aspects of the hidden perception of the traumatic situation. The fear of oblivion can be worked around by treating aspects.

Kinesthetic and proprioceptive memories also play an important role in the treatment of childhood trauma. The perception of the perpetrator's body – body weight, hands, mouth, genitals – is frozen at the moment of the boundary transgressions. This, as well as the perception of the child's own body, leads to the creation of frozen energy structures that can be activated. When this happens, the emotions and body sensations are reactivated. The traumatic event is then re-experienced directly and projected on people who are present in the here-and-now. A loving husband can become a perpetrator of the past.

There is also the aspect of the frozen perception of the client's own body. If the abuse happened at the age of four, a frozen energy structure of the client's body at that age is created and stored. This energy structure has a kinesthetic/proprioceptive content and is usually contained within the space of the client's adult body. In most cases, this frozen energy structure hides the adult awareness of the client's body, with the strength and flexibility of the latter. To restore the awareness of the adult body we can use Logosynthesis on the frozen energy structure of the child body.

SEXUAL ABUSE
TRAUMA
CHILDHOOD

THE DARK SHADOW IN THE LIGHT

Catherine said: "I'm scared, but the time is ripe." She wanted to take a next step in the processing of a deep wound from her youth. She had a memory that, as a fourteen-year-old, the door of her bedroom opened, and a dark shadow stood in the light that came through the door; then her memory went blank. The next day she had gone to school, and she knew that her life would never be the same. Something terrible had happened, but she wasn't aware what it had been.

As there was no other story to tell, and because I had worked with Catherine before, I could immediately give her the first sentence for the image of the dark shadow standing in the light of the doorway. After this sentence, she said: "I wish my mother had been there to protect me." I gave her the first and second Logosynthesis sentence for that wish, and she seemed to relax. However, when I gave her the third sentence "I retrieve all my energy, bound up in all my reactions to the fact that my mother didn't protect me," she was visibly overwhelmed by the pain of the memory.

She said, in tears: "I feel so alone." When I quietly asked what made her feel so alone, she said that her mouth was "occupied" and that she could not speak. To not interrupt the flow of the process and support her in this state of utter loneliness, I decided to say the sentences on her behalf, for what had been occupying her mouth. That brought an enormous relief, and it became clear what it was that occupied her mouth: She had been orally raped. Catherine said, angrily, but also relieved: "Such a damned pig!"

Now it almost seemed that the work was finished. To check for any remaining introjects, I asked Catherine to tell me the story again, from the moment the man entered the room until the time he left. This reactivated another layer, and she remembered vividly the feel of semen running from her mouth down her cheeks. Again, I said the three sentences on her behalf, and she was able to process the experience in minutes. She said that it felt at the same time completely unknown and disgusting. She had had no previous sexual experience with a man before this incident.

There is no way to avoid the fact that children are abused in this world, but Logosynthesis can be very helpful to cope with and process the trauma of sexual abuse. For that, it's very important that there be a strong working alliance.

SEXUAL ABUSE
WORKING ALLIANCE
MEMORIES

RESOLVING INCOMPETENCE

Kathy had a deep belief that she was incompetent. She had been offering counseling sessions for free, even as a child she had been painfully shy, and her mother called her "sickly sensitive." She hadn't felt safe in her family growing up, was afraid of others, and felt like an outsider. Her birth had been an "accident" as her parents hadn't used contraceptives. She had been sexually abused by her father.

I decided to explore the sexual abuse issue, because neutralizing such events can free an enormous amount of life energy.

Kathy had worked on the issue before, but it was still active. She had scraps of a scene in the bathroom with her father and also remembered that her father had held her head in the toilet bowl. I asked her for the most disturbing aspect of the abuse. She couldn't answer that question, so I followed my intuition and decided to start with the bathroom scene.

She reported that she wanted to hide. She felt ashamed and dirty remembering that scene. She saw herself from above, in the bathtub with her father near her. I gave her the first Logosynthesis sentence for the image of these two people, as I always do when a client has an image in which it seems they have left their body. Usually the client will access the experience from the perspective of being inside their body after that first sentence, but that can be very painful.

This time after the first sentence Kathy had another image, still from outside of herself, of the little girl in the bathtub, but this time closer to her head, and she could see the bathtub as a whole. I gave her the first sentence again. After that she accessed her body experience of the event, and strong abdominal pains came up. She also saw the eyes of her father. I decided to not elicit further details and gave her the sentences for "the image of the eyes of my father and everything it represents." She cried tears of relief. She felt more grounded and felt herself growing in the scene: She became the adult woman she is now, looking at the scene of the little girl and her father. I once again offered her the sentences for this image, and she told me that she felt less tension in her body. She said: "Life doesn't have to be such an effort."

To complete the work, I addressed the second scene, in which her father had held her head in the toilet bowl. Kathy said: "If I think about it, I could kill him." It was clear that her energy level had been raised by processing the first memory. I asked her if she could process this herself with the help of Logosynthesis, and she confirmed this. She looked great now, gleaming with self-confidence and ready to tackle life's challenges. There remained not a trace of the timid woman at the beginning of the session.

We often see the same stages in the treatment of childhood sexual abuse with Logosynthesis:

> 1. In the interview scraps of an experience show up. This experience often contains images from a perspective in which the client has left their physical body. If the images are too confronting, the subconscious of the client can produce metaphors, like pigs, or rats crawling over or entering the body.

2. The Logosynthesis sentence 1 for such an image causes the client to access the experience from inside the body, with direct input from their senses. In this case, the first sentence was used twice to achieve this. Entering the body is often associated with great physical pain, the reason why the client left their body in the first place.

3. At this stage the environment is explored using the senses and the memories of the sensory input are neutralized with the help of the Logosynthesis sentences. If there is a partial memory, the words "and everything this represents," can be added to the description of the trigger in the sentences.

4. The result is deep relief and a reconnection to the awareness of the adult person in the present.

▓
SEXUAL ABUSE
CHILDHOOD
IMAGES

INDEX

ACCIDENT
16, 19, 34, 35, 42, 46, 71

BELIEFS
34, 40, 43, 49, 52, 53, 54, 73

CHILDHOOD
39, 42, 46, 75, 76, 79, 80, 82, 86, 92, 96

CHILDREN
53, 87

EMOTIONS
43, 54, 58, 69, 71, 76

ESSENCE
22, 46, 65

FAMILY OF ORIGIN
24, 42, 52, 62, 64, 72, 73, 75, 76, 77, 79, 84, 86, 89

FANTASIES
38, 58

HEALTH AND ILLNESS
14, 16, 18, 19, 20, 22, 23, 24, 26, 34, 39, 44

IMAGES
23, 26, 35, 38, 53, 72, 73, 80, 96

LIFE TRANSITIONS
35, 44, 54, 56, 60, 62, 82

MEMORIES
14, 16, 18, 20, 23, 43, 54, 64, 69, 90, 94

MISSION
51, 62, 87

PARENTS
14, 18, 20, 24, 51, 52, 69, 71, 79, 80, 82, 86

PARTNERSHIP
30, 40, 54

ROMANCE
30, 40, 54

SEXUAL ABUSE
90, 92, 94, 96

SOCIOENERGETIC FIELDS
22, 75

TRAUMA
29, 30, 38, 44, 72, 84, 92

WISHES AND DESIRES
29, 39, 58, 60, 77

WORK
19, 29, 56, 60, 65, 77, 84

WORKING ALLIANCE
26, 56, 64, 65, 90, 94

Notes

Notes

Notes

Notes

Printed in Great Britain
by Amazon